Harvard Economic Studies, Volume 149

Awarded the David A. Wells Prize for the year 1976 and published from the income of the David A. Wells Fund.

The studies in this series are published under the direction of the Department of Economics of Harvard University. The Department does not assume responsibility for the views expressed.

Essays in the Economics of Uncertainty

Jean-Jacques Laffont

HARVARD UNIVERSITY PRESS

Cambridge, Massachusetts
and London, England
1980

Copyright © 1980 by the President and
Fellows of Harvard College
All rights reserved
Printed in the United States of America

Library of Congress Cataloging in Publication Data

Laffont, Jean Jacques.
  Essays in the economics of uncertainty.

  (Harvard economic studies; v. 149)
  Bibliography: p.
  Includes index.
  1. Uncertainty—Mathematical models.   I. Title.
II. Series.
HB615.125   330.1   79-19771
ISBN 0-674-26555-6

Preface

The success of a paradigm . . . is at the start largely a promise of success discoverable in selected and still incomplete examples. Normal science consists in the actualization of that promise, an actualization achieved by extending the knowledge of those facts that the paradigm displays as particularly revealing, by increasing the extent of the match between those facts and the paradigm's prediction, and by further articulation of the paradigm itself.

Thomas S. Kuhn, *The Structure of Scientific Revolutions*

In this book, I accept the neoclassical paradigm as a useful framework for dealing with questions of uncertainty. I do not pretend to solve an economic problem. I only address questions raised in very special models chosen for their meaningfulness, but also for their convenience. At most, I am engaged in normal science, with all its limitations. However, I hope to do a little more than "bring our problem to a conclusion by achieving the anticipated in a new way which requires the solution of all sorts of complex instrumental, conceptual, and mathematical puzzles" (Kuhn 1962).

I hope to focus on an important but neglected problem and to reveal sometimes unexpected results. I hope to take a small but definite step toward a better understanding of the role of uncertainty in economics. An important dimension of economic behavior has not received the attention it deserves. Namely, that economic agents can often have an impact on the probability distributions they face.

When the probability distributions are subjective, any attempt to sharpen these distributions, to improve one's information, can be considered part of the problem. In this case the basic uncertainty is unchanged, but new information can lead to different outcomes. My interest is characterizing the consequences of information availability. At this stage of economic science a very general study of this question seems unlikely to be fruitful. On the contrary, relatively specific models are needed to tackle this question. The purpose of part I is to assess the consequences of information availability in a general equilibrium model with asymmetrical information on the quality of products.

When the probability distributions are objective, an economic impact on them is better viewed as an attempt to modify the basic uncertainty of the economy by the use of economic instruments. Part II provides a general equilibrium analysis of this phenomenon in an economy endowed with an insurance system that has usually been referred to as creating a moral hazard.

In part III I show that important results of the bounded rationality literature, namely, results on certainty equivalence, have to be modified to account for the use of economic instruments to modify (subjective or objective) uncertainty.

I am very grateful to Kenneth Arrow and Jerry Green, whose kindness and intellectual support made the writing of this book a most enjoyable experience.

I also benefited from discussions with Truman Bewley and with my fellow graduate students Elhanan Helpman and Vince FitzGerald. Finally, I would like to thank Tom Barthold for reviewing the completed manuscript.

The *Journal of Economic Theory,* the *Journal of Mathematical Economics,* the *Review of Economic Studies,* and *Economica* kindly authorized the use of material that they first published.

Contents

PART I
Exchange with Asymmetrical Information

In Part I, I consider an exchange model with asymmetrical information. Buyers do not know the quality of the goods they are buying, while sellers of these commodities are well aware of it. In chapter 1, I develop a general equilibrium theory both in the short run and in the long run for such an economy. The role of expectations and in particular of optimism of expectations is emphasized. Then information acquisition is made available to uninformed agents in the form of experts able to identify the quality of commodities.

The analysis is then pursued in a game theory framework. An attempt is made to adapt the concept of core to this situation of asymmetrical information.

Finally, some comments on the use of ethical changes to attack this informational problem are made in an appendix.

1

Optimism and Experts against Adverse Selection in a Competitive Economy

Pareto optimality of competitive equilibrium is obtained at the cost of the necessary existence of a large number of markets, especially when future periods or uncertainty is considered. Transaction costs as well as institutional constraints usually prevent the setting up of a sufficient number of markets to guarantee Pareto optimality. Consequently a fundamental problem in economic theory is the description and the study of a competitive economy without a complete set of markets. Externalities have been analyzed as a lack of markets; the concept of noncooperative equilibrium has been proposed as a description, and internalization of externalities by the creation of missing markets has been suggested to solve the problem. Recent models of temporary equilibrium (Grandmont 1973) assume a lack of future markets and restrict their study of efficiency to stationary states (Grandmont and Younès 1972). Malinvaud (1973) studies the problem of individual risks in which a reduced set of markets may perform very well.

The existence of markets for all goods and dates creates a symmetry of information about the objects of trade for buyers and sellers. This is not necessarily true in the case of contingent markets; people do not need to agree on probabilities of future events to obtain Pareto optimality or at least ex ante optimality. Starr (1973) recently demonstrated the conditions under which some homogeneity of expectations is sufficient to obtain ex post optimality. However, even in this case, people know perfectly the characteristics of goods that they buy or sell. Indeed, the assumption that sellers generally know what they are selling seems reasonable, but the same assumption about buyers is not always satisfied when imperfect information prevails. There are at least two sources of imperfect information about products. First, without consuming, people may not know how to assess the well-defined characteristics of goods, particularly new goods, but this source of imperfect information is relatively unimportant in the long run. The main source of imperfect information is that both good and bad products are sold on the same market without meaningful brands or signals to distinguish the good from the bad. For example, both ripe and overripe oranges are sold as oranges and both good and bad used cars are sold as used cars.

In this chapter, I am interested in commodities whose intrinsic differences are known to "dishonest" sellers but are not perceptible by buyers. A short-run equilibrium concept to describe economies with such goods is defined. Under certain conditions such a short-run equilibrium can be shown to exist, and Akerlof's (1970) predicted breakdown of markets can be avoided (appendix 1.A gives Akerlof's example). Moreover there is a long-run equilibrium in which expectations about qualities are fulfilled. Costly information can be made available to consumers in the form of experts who are able to perceive qualities of goods, but the introduction of experts may be inefficient.

A Concept of Short-Run Competitive Equilibrium

Consider a competitive exchange economy with $L + 2$ goods and n consumers. The first L commodities, indexed by $l = 1, \ldots, L$, are the usual commodities sold on L different markets. Commodities $L + 1, L + 2$, also called good *y* and good *z*, are sold on a unique market, market $L + 1$.[1] Sellers of goods *y* and *z* can discriminate between them but buyers cannot, so each purchase is a gamble whose outcome is a proportion of goods *y* and *z*. We refer to the melange when talking about what is sold in market $L + 1$. Good *y* and good *z* can be two qualities of the same commodity, for example. One interesting special case occurs when good *y* or good *z* is not desired; we may then have Akerlof's problem; that is, the desired commodity is driven out of the market by the undesired one. More precisely, the breakdown of market $L + 1$ occurs when the equilibrium price of the melange is zero and no exchange of the desired good *y* or *z* occurs. Under certain conditions this breakdown can be avoided. In fact, there are conditions under which the equilibrium price of the melange is nonzero.

Let $w^i = (w_x^i, w_y^i, w_z^i) \in R_+^L \times R_+ \times R_+$ be the vector of endowments in goods $l = 1, \ldots, L$, good *y*, good *z* respectively, of consumer $i, i = 1, \ldots, n$. Let $y^i (z^i)$ be the quantity of good *y* (*z*) that consumer *i* consumes, and let v^i be the quantity of melange that he buys from market $L + 1$. His consumption set is R_+^{L+2}, but in this problem it does not define his choice space.

Let $\pi = (p, q) \in S \times R_+$ be the price vector of this exchange economy, where *S* is the simplex of R^L, *p* the price vector of goods $1, \ldots, L$, and *q* the price of the melange.

Consumer *i* then faces uncertainty concerning the proportion of good *y* that he can expect from a purchase on market $L + 1$. Assume that he has a subjective probability distribution on this proportion θ, which depends on prices and on the quantity of melange he purchases; in other words, he has an expectation function ψ^i that associates with each (π, v^i) a probability measure on the unit interval $\Delta = [0, 1]$. The expectation function ψ^i is then a mapping from $S \times R_+ \times R_+$ into the space $\mathcal{M}(\Delta)$ of probability measures on Δ. The space

---

1. For simplicity, we limit the number of goods sold on market $L + 1$ to two, but the analysis can be carried out with any finite number of goods.

$S \times R_+ \times R_+$ is endowed with the usual topology, $\mathcal{M}(\Delta)$ with the weak topology. The image of (π, v^i) under the mapping ψ^i is denoted by $\psi^i(\cdot, \pi, v^i)$.

Assumption 1. The mapping ψ^i is continuous from $S \times R_+ \times R_+$ into $\mathcal{M}(\Delta)$, $i = 1, \ldots, n$.

For each equilibrium price vector π, there is a market proportion of good y, $\bar{\theta}(\pi)$. The buyer is not only ignorant of this relation but is also subject to a random process that determines his own proportion θ, given $\bar{\theta}$. For a short-run analysis it is not necessary to specify this process more precisely.

The dependence of ψ^i on purchases is due to the following statistical mechanism. There is a proportion $\bar{\theta}$ in the market. If the agent randomly buys unit after unit from the market population, the variance of his θ will decrease with the quantity bought.

Competitive behavior has two meanings here. First, agents have a parametric behavior with respect to prices. Second, sellers of melange believe that they can affect neither the true market proportion nor the buyers' expectations about the market proportion.

Assumption 2. Each consumer, $i = 1, \ldots, n$, has a continuous, bounded, concave Von Neumann utility function u^i from R_+^{L+2} into R.

The maximization problem of consumer i can therefore be written[2]

$$\text{Max } U^i(x^i, y^i, z^i, v^i, \pi)$$
$$= \int_\Delta u^i(x^i, y^i + \theta v^i, z^i + (1 - \theta)v^i)d\psi^i(\theta, \pi, v^i)$$

---

2. We use the following convention for inequalities between vectors, where $x \in R^n$, $y \in R^n$.

$x > y$ means $x_l > y_l$, $l = 1, \ldots, n$;

$x \geq y$ means $x_l \geq y_l$, $l = 1, \ldots, n$, with at least one strict inequality;

$x \geqq y$ means $x_l \geqq y_l$, $l = 1, \ldots, n$.

subject to

$$px^i + qv^i \leq pw^i_x + q(w^i_y - y^i) + q(w^i_z - z^i),$$
$$x^i, y^i, z^i, v^i \geq 0; \quad y^i \leq w^i_y; \quad z^i \leq w^i_z.$$

An action $a^i = (x^i, y^i, z^i, v^i)$ is feasible if it is technically feasible—that is, if $a^i \in A^i = \{(x, y, z, v)|x, y, z, v \geq 0, y \leq w^i_y, z \leq w^i_z\}$—and satisfies the budget constraint

$$a^i \in \Gamma^i(\pi) = \{x, y, z, v|px + q(v + y + z)$$
$$\leq pw^i_x + q(w^i_y + w^i_z)\}.$$

Assumption 3. For each $i = 1, \ldots, n$ the following properties hold.

1. $w^i_x > 0$.

2. $x \geq x', y \geq y', z \geq z'$ implies $u^i(x, y, z) \geq u^i(x', y', z'); x \geq x'$ implies $u^i(x, y, z) > u^i(x', y, z)$ for all $y, z \in R_+$; and $y > y'$ implies $u^i(x, y, z) > u^i(x, y', z)$ for all $x \in R^L_+$, all $z \in R_+$, or $z > z'$ implies $u^i(x, y, z) > u^i(x, y, z')$ for all $x \in R^L_+$, all $y \in R_+$.

Assumption 4. A consumer i satisfies the following properties:

1. $w^i_y + w^i_z > 0$.

2. When he desires good y, there exists $\epsilon > 0$ and $\eta > 0$ such that

$$\int_0^\epsilon d\psi^i(\theta, \pi, v^i) < 1 - \eta \quad \text{for all } \pi \in S \times R_+, \text{ all } v^i \in R_+.$$

or when he desires good z, there exists $\epsilon > 0$ and $\eta > 0$ such that

$$\int_{1-\epsilon}^1 d\psi^i(\theta, \pi, v^i) < 1 - \eta \quad \text{for all } \pi \in S \times R_+, \text{ all } v^i \in R_+.$$

The second part of this assumption requires agent i to believe that the proportion in the melange of the good he desires is always positive with positive probability. Agent i is optimistic.

The notation $a >_i a'$ means $[x \geq x', \text{ and } v \geq v', y \geq y', z \geq z']$ or $[x \geq x', z \geq z', \text{ and } (y > y' \text{ and } v \geq v') \text{ or } (y \geq y' \text{ and}$

$v > v'$) if consumer *i* desires good *y*] or [$x \geq x'$ and $y \geq y'$ and
($z > z'$ and $v \geq v'$) or ($z \geq z'$ and $v > v'$) if consumer *i* desires good *z*].

A *short-run competitive quasi equilibrium* is a price vector
$\pi^* \in S \times R_+$ and a set of actions $a^{*1}, \ldots, a^{*n}$ such that

$$U^i(a^{*i}, \pi^*) = \text{Max } U^i(a, \pi^*), \qquad a \in A^i \cap \Gamma^i(\pi^*), \quad (1.1)$$

for $i = 1, \ldots, n$ with the possible exception of $L + 1$ consumers (*n* is assumed larger than $L + 1$) for whom the action
belongs only to the convex hull of the action correspondence

$$\sum_{i=1}^{n} x^{*i} \leq \sum_{i=1}^{n} w_x^i \quad \text{and} \quad p\left(\sum_{i=1}^{n} x^{*i} - \sum_{i=1}^{n} w_x^i\right) = 0;$$

$$\sum_{i=1}^{n} (v^{*i} + y^{*i} + z^{*i}) \leq \sum_{i=1}^{n} (w_y^i + w_z^i), \quad \text{and}$$

$$q\left[\sum_{i=1}^{n} (v^{*i} + y^{*i} + z^{*i} - w_y^i - w_z^i)\right] = 0. \qquad (1.2)$$

If the qualification in equation 1.1 concerning the $L + 1$
consumers is suppressed, the quasi equilibrium is called an
equilibrium. If *n* is large with respect to $L + 1$, a quasi equilibrium is almost an equilibrium.

By a sequence of lemmas I prove the existence of a
short-run competitive quasi equilibrium where the melange
has a positive price.

Lemma 1.   The function U^i is continuous on $A^i \times S \times R_+$,
$i = 1, \ldots, n$.

Proof.   Let $(a_0, \pi_0) \in A^i \times S \times R_+$ and (a_j, π_j) be a sequence in $A^i \times S \times R_+$ converging to (a_0, π_0). The sequence
of functions $u^i(x_j, y_j + \cdot v_j, z_j + (1 - \cdot)v_j)$ from Δ into R is uniformly bounded (assumption 2) and converges continuously
to $u^i(x_0, y_0 + \cdot v_0, z_0 + (1 - \cdot)v_0)$, since u^i is continuous with
respect to all variables. By assumption 1, $\psi^i(\cdot, \pi_j, v_j)$ is a sequence of measures that converges weakly to $\psi^i(\cdot, \pi_0, v_0)$.
Therefore, according to Grandmont (1972, theorem A3,
sect. 5), $\lim_j U^i(a_j, \pi_j) = U^i(a_0, \pi_0)$.   QED

Lemma 2. Given $\pi \in S \times R_+$, the function $U^i(\cdot, \pi)$ is continuous and increasing in a (in the sense of $>_i$), $i = 1, \ldots, n$.

Proof. The proof is obvious from assumptions 2 and 3 and the definition of U^i.

Let $P = \{\pi = (p, q) | \pi \in S \times R_+, \pi > 0\}$. Let $\hat{\Gamma}^i(\pi) = A^i \cap \Gamma^i(\pi)$ be the budget correspondence of consumer i, and let $\xi^i(\pi)$ be the action correspondence of consumer i, for $i = 1, \ldots, n$.

Lemma 3. The budget correspondence $\hat{\Gamma}^i$ is a continuous mapping, with nonempty, convex, compact values, from P into R_+^{L+3}.

Proof. By assumption 3, $\hat{\Gamma}^i$ is continuous (Debreu 1959). The application of lemma 3.10 of Green (1971), and assumption 2, gives the result.

Lemma 4. The action correspondence ξ^i is a nonempty, compact-valued, and upper hemicontinuous (uhc) mapping from P into R_+^{L+3}, and the budget constraint of agent i is binding, for $i = 1, \ldots, n$.

Proof. The first part is obtained by the maximum theorem, and the second part from assumption 3.

Lemma 5. Consider a consumer i who satisfies assumption 4. Let π_j be a sequence in P and a_j a sequence in $\xi^i(\pi_j)$. If $\pi_j \to S \times R_+ \backslash P$ or $q \to \infty$, then $|a_j| \to \infty$.

Proof. Assume that the sequence a_j is bounded; then there exists a subsequence (same notation) that converges to a_0. The space $\mathcal{M}(\Delta)$ is compact, since Δ is compact (Parthasarathy 1967, chap. 2, theorem 6.4). From the sequence $\psi^i(\cdot, \pi_j, v_j)$ in the compact space $\mathcal{M}(\Delta)$, we can extract a subsequence (same notation) converging weakly to $\psi^i_0(\cdot) \in \mathcal{M}(\Delta)$. Let $I^i(a) = \int_\Delta u^i(x, y + \cdot v, z + (1 - \cdot)v) d\psi^i_0(\cdot)$. Since u^i is continuous and bounded, $U^i(a, \pi_j) = \int_\Delta u^i(x, y + \cdot v, z + (1 - $

$\cdot)v)d\psi^i(\cdot, \pi_j, v_j)$ converges to $I^i(a)$ as j goes to infinity. From theorem A3 of Grandmont (1972, sect. 5), $U^i(a_j, \pi_j)$ converges to $U^i(a_0, \pi_0)$ as j goes to infinity. Moreover $I^i(a)$ is continuous by the dominated convergence theorem, since u^i is continuous and bounded and ψ^i is a probability measure on the compact set Δ.

a. If $\pi_j \to S \times R_+\backslash P$ and $p_j \to \bar{S}$,

$$U^i(a_j, \pi_j) \geq U^i(a, \pi_j)$$

for all $a \in \hat{\Gamma}^i(\pi_j)$, by definition of a_j;

$$p_0 x_0 + q_0(v_0 + y_0 + z_0) \leq p_0 w_x^i + q_0(w_y^i + w_z^i).$$

By assumption 3, $p_0 w_x^i > 0$. Then for all $a = (x, v, y, z) \in \hat{\Gamma}^i(\pi_0)$, take $\lambda \in [0, 1)$ such that

$$p_0 \lambda x + q_0 \lambda(v + y + z) < p_0 w_x^i + q_0(w_y^i + w_z^i).$$

Thus for j large enough

$$p_j \lambda x + q_j \lambda(v + y + z) < p_j w_x^i + q_j(w_y^i + w_z^i).$$

Therefore $U^i(\lambda a, \pi_j) < U^i(a_j, \pi_j)$. Letting j go to infinity, gives $I^i(\lambda a) \leq I^i(a_0)$, and letting λ go to one gives $I^i(a) \leq I^i(a_0)$, by the continuity of I^i. But $I^i(a_0) \geq I^i(a)$ for all $a \in \hat{\Gamma}^i(\pi_0)$ is contradicted by the existence of $k \in [1, \ldots, L]$ such that $p_{0k} = 0$ and by assumption 3.

b. If $\pi_j \to S \times R_+\backslash P$ and $q_j \to 0$, the same argument leads to $I^i(a_0) \geq I^i(a)$ for all $a \in \hat{\Gamma}^i(\pi_0)$. By the second part of assumption 4 this is a contradiction, since v goes to infinity if $q_0 = 0$.

If $q_j \to \infty$, then $I^i(a_0) \geq I(a)$ for all $a = (x, y_0, z_0, v_0)$ with x arbitrary. Dividing the budget constraint by q_j gives

$$\frac{p_j}{q_j} \cdot x_j + (y_j + z_j + v_j) \leq \frac{p_j}{q_j} w_x^i + (w_j^i + w_z^i),$$

and taking the limit gives

$$(y_0 + z_0 + v_0) \leq w_y^i + w_z^i.$$

By the first part of assumption 4 we have $w_y^i + w_z^i > 0$. Let $\lambda \in [0, 1)$. Then $\lambda(y_0 + z_0 + v_0) < w_y^i + w_z^i$. For j large enough

$$\frac{p_j \lambda x}{q_j} + \lambda(y_0 + z_0 + v_0) < \frac{p_j}{q_j} w_x^i + (w_y^i + w_z^i)$$

or

$$\lambda p_j x + \lambda q_j(y_0 + z_0 + v_0) < p_j w_x^i + q_j(w_y^i + w_z^i).$$

Then

$$U^i(\lambda x, \lambda y_0, \lambda z_0, \lambda v_0, \pi_j) \lesseqgtr U^i(a_j, \pi_j).$$

If we let j go to infinity, we have

$$U^i(\lambda x, \lambda y_0, \lambda z_0, \lambda v_0, \pi_0) \lesseqgtr U^i(a_0, \pi_0).$$

If we let λ go to one, then by the continuity of $I^i(a)$ we obtain

$$I^i(a) \lesseqgtr I^i(a_0).$$

But if $a = (x', y_0, z_0, v_0)$ with $x' \geq x_0$, then $I^i(a) > I^i(a_0)$; hence we have a contradiction.   QED

Theorem 1.1.   Consider an economy that satisfies assumptions 1–3 and in which one consumer satisfies assumption 4. Then there exists a short-run, competitive quasi equilibrium with a strictly positive price vector.

Proof.   For each $\pi \in P$, let

$$\zeta(\pi) = \begin{bmatrix} \displaystyle\sum_{i=1}^{n} (x^i(\pi) - w_x^i) \\ \displaystyle\sum_{i=1}^{n} (y^i(\pi) + z^i(\pi) + v^i(\pi) - w_y^i - w_z^i) \end{bmatrix}$$

be the aggregate excess-demand correspondence. It satisfies the assumptions of Grandmont's theorem 1 (1973, appendix) except that it is not convex valued. Consider con $\zeta(\pi)$. Con $\zeta(\pi)$ is uhc with nonempty, convex, compact values (Hildenbrand, 1974, proposition 6). All assumptions of Grandmont's theorem 1 (1973, appendix) are satisfied for con $\zeta(\pi)$. Then there exists a price "equilibrium" in P for con $\zeta(\pi)$. Finally, Starr's lemma 2 (1969, p. 35) gives the result.   QED

If the expectation functions do not depend on the quantity of melange purchased, then U^i is concave; indeed u^i is concave in (x^i, y^i, z^i, v^i) as a composition of linear functions and of a concave function $u^i(\cdot, \cdot, \cdot)$. The demand correspondences are therefore convex valued, and theorem 1.1 gives the existence of an equilibrium.

Let us compare our analysis with Akerlof's example. The basic difference is that Akerlof assumes that buyers of melange know the market proportion of good y as a function of price. With uncertainty in the market this assumption appears unsatisfactory. Our analysis assumes only that consumers have expectations about this relation. In such a world we found a weak assumption (4) that with other standard assumptions insures the existence of an equilibrium without a breakdown of the market for melange. Assumption 4 expresses the idea that one consumer is superoptimistic; he never believes that the proportion of the desired good in the melange is zero with probability one or that his expectations are inelastic around a positive value of this proportion.

An assumption like 4 is acceptable for describing a dynamic economy if the equilibrium path is viewed as a sequence of short-run equilibria that are only loosely connected, with new agents appearing each period. In a static world, where endowments and preferences are identical each period, a revision of expectations may drive any superoptimism from the economy. Then Akerlof's result may appear as a long-run equilibrium in a static economy.

Long-Run Equilibrium

To simplify this section we assume that the expectation functions depend only on prices. We have shown that for any given set of continuous expectation functions $\Phi = \{\Psi^1(\theta, \cdot), \ldots, \Psi^n(\theta, \cdot)\}$, there exists a short-run competitive equilibrium. Consumers, after consuming and gathering information at a short-run equilibrium, will revise their expectations. A long-run equilibrium will be a state of the economy such that the revision process leads to the same expectations and then to the same short-run equilibrium in all future periods. Let us define more precisely the uncertainty faced by consumers.

The market proportion $\bar{\theta}$ of good y in the melange depends on the price system π and on the set of expectation functions Φ. Each consumer has a prior distribution on $\bar{\theta}$ for each price vector $h^i(\bar{\theta}, \pi)$, but he cannot appreciate its dependence on Φ. Then if the market proportion is $\bar{\theta}$, a stochastic process determines the proportion θ obtained by a consumer. Let $\mu(\cdot|\bar{\theta})$ be the measure that summarizes this process, and assume that it is known to consumers. The expectation function of consumer i is then deduced from the convolution of these distributions.

$$\Psi^i(\cdot, \pi) = \int_\Delta \mu(\cdot|\bar{\theta})h^i(d\bar{\theta}, \pi), \qquad i = 1, \ldots, n.$$

The measure $\mu(\cdot|\bar{\theta})$ can be regarded as given by the market structure. The revision process operates basically on h^i and gives new Ψ^i by combination with $\mu(\cdot|\bar{\theta})$.

However, we shall use a cruder revision process. Assume that at the end of each period consumers know the short-run equilibrium price vector π_t and the market proportion $\bar{\theta}_t$ of good y. They revise their expectation functions according to the process

$$\Psi^i_{t+1}(\cdot, \cdot) = H^i[\Psi^i_t(\cdot, \cdot), \bar{\theta}_t, \pi_t], \qquad i = 1, \ldots, n.$$

We use a new normalization of prices.

$$S = \{(p, q) = \pi \,\Big|\, \sum_{k=1}^{L} p_k + q = 1, q, p_k \geqq 0, k = 1, \ldots, L.\}$$

The expectation function $\Psi^i(\cdot, \cdot)$ is a mapping from S into $\mathcal{M}(\Delta)$. Let $\mathcal{C}$ be the space of continuous functions from S into $\mathcal{M}(\Delta)$. We endow $\mathcal{C}$ with the compact open topology (Kelley 1955), which is the weakest topology such that if $\pi_j \to \pi^*$ and $\Psi_j(\cdot, \pi) \to \Psi^*(\cdot, \pi)$ in the compact open topology, then $\Psi_j(\cdot, \pi_j) \to \Psi^*(\cdot, \pi^*)$ in the weak topology.

Now U^i is also considered a function of $\Psi^i(\cdot, \cdot)$.

We consider a sequence of short-run equilibria. During each period consumers (who live forever) have the same endowments and the same Von Neumann utility functions.

A *long-run competitive equilibrium* is a price system $\pi^* \in S$, a market proportion $\bar{\theta}^*$, a set of actions $(a^{*1}, \ldots, a^{*n})$, and a set of expectation functions $[\Psi^{*1}(\cdot, \pi), \ldots, \Psi^{*n}(\cdot, \pi)]$ such that

$$\Psi^{*i}(\cdot, \pi^*) = H^i[\Psi^{*i}(\cdot, \pi^*), \theta^*, \pi^*], \quad \text{for } i = 1, \ldots, n;$$

$$U^i(a^{*i}, \pi^*, \Psi^{*i}) = \text{Max } U^i(a, \pi^*, \Psi^{*i}), \quad a \in \hat{\Gamma}^i(\pi^*);$$

$$\sum_{i=1}^{n} x^{*i} \leq \sum_{i=1}^{n} w_x^i \quad \text{with } p^* \left(\sum_{i=1}^{n} x^{*i} - \sum_{i=1}^{n} w_x^i \right) = 0,$$

$$\sum_{i=1}^{n} (y^{*i} + z^{*i} + v^{*i}) \leq \sum_{i=1}^{n} (w_y^i + w_z^i),$$

$$\text{with } q^* \left[\sum_{i=1}^{n} (y^{*i} + z^{*i} + v^{*i} - w_y^i - w_z^i) \right] = 0.$$

Note that we require the expectation functions to be stationary only for the equilibrium price π^* and not for all values of π.

Assumption 5. The revision process H^i is continuous from $\mathscr{C} \times \Delta \times S$ into $\mathscr{C}$, $i = 1, \ldots, n$.
Recall that $U^i(a, \pi, \Psi^i) = \int_\Delta u^i(x, y + \theta v, z + (1 - \theta)v)d\Psi^i(\theta, \pi)$.

Lemma 6. The mapping U^i is continuous from $A^i \times S \times \mathscr{C}$ into R, $i = 1, \ldots, n$.

Proof. Let us consider sequences $a_j \to a$, $\pi_j \to \pi$, $\Psi_j^i \to \Psi^i$. From the joint continuity, we know that $\Psi_j^i(\theta, \pi_j) \to \Psi^i(\theta, \pi)$ in the weak topology. Since $u^i(x_j, y_j + \theta v_j, z_j + (1 - \theta)v_j)$ converges continuously to $u^i(x, y + \theta v, z + (1 - \theta)v)$ and is uniformly bounded, we can again use Grandmont's theorem A3 (1973, section 5) to obtain that $U^i(a_j, \pi_j, \Psi_j^i)$ converges to $U^i(a, \pi, \Psi^i)$. QED

We use the Arrow-Debreu (1954) technical compactification method.[3]

Lemma 7. Under assumptions 1–3, 4.1, and 5 the truncated action correspondence $\bar{a}^i(\pi, \Psi^i)$, $i = 1, \ldots, n$, is upper hemicontinuous with nonempty, convex values from $S \times \mathscr{C}$ into a fixed compact set.

Proof. The result is obtained by the maximum theorem, and the fixed compact set is the compact ball C defined as in Arrow and Debreu (1954).   QED

Let $D = \Pi_{i=1}^n [0, w_y^i] \times \Pi_{i=1}^n [0, w_z^i]$. The market proportion of good y is a function of actions taken by consumers. Let λ_θ be the correspondence from D into Δ defined as follows.

If $\Sigma_{i=1}^n w_y^i = \Sigma_{i=1}^n y^i$ and $\Sigma_{i=1}^n w_z^i = \Sigma_{i=1}^n z^i$,

$$\lambda_\theta(y^1, \ldots, y^n, z^1, \ldots, z^n) = [0, 1];$$

otherwise

$$\lambda_\theta(y^1, \ldots, y^n, z^1, \ldots, z^n) = \frac{\Sigma_{i=1}^n (w_y^i - y^i)}{\Sigma_{i=1}^n (w_y^i - y^i) + \Sigma_{i=1}^n (w_z^i - z^i)}.$$

The correspondence λ_θ is obviously nonempty, compact, convex valued, and uhc.

We identify a probability measure on Δ, $\mu^i(\theta)$ with a constant expectation function $\Psi^i(\theta, \pi)$ such that $\Psi^i(\theta, \pi) = \mu^i(\theta)$ for all $\pi \in S$. To each measure $\mu^i(\theta)$ we associate a new measure λ^i in the following way. To μ^i viewed as a constant expectation function we associate by H^i a new expectation function. We take the value of this expectation function at π, and we consider the constant expectation function that has this

---

3. Let C be a compact ball containing the feasible set in its interior. We intersect the action space of consumers $\hat{\Gamma}^i(\pi)$ with C. Let $\tilde{\Gamma}^i(\pi) = C \cap \hat{\Gamma}^i(\pi)$. The truncated action correspondence $\bar{a}^i(\pi, \Psi^i)$ is the action correspondence defined on $\tilde{\Gamma}^i(\pi)$. We first show the existence of a fixed point for the truncated economy; then using the concavity of V^i, we show that the fixed point is an equilibrium.

value. By assumption 5, λ^i is obviously continuous from $\mathscr{C}_R$ into $\mathscr{C}_R$, where $\mathscr{C}_R$ is the subset of constant functions in $\mathscr{C}$.

Now consider an auctioneer who maximizes $p\zeta$ in S, where ζ is the excess demand on the $L + 1$ markets (ζ is a continuous function of (x^i, y^i, z^i, v^i), $i = 1, \ldots, n$, into R^{L+1}).

Let λ_π be the correspondence that associates to each (x^i, y^i, z^i, v^i), $i = 1, \ldots, n$, the set of maximizing prices. It is an upper hemicontinuous nonempty, convex, compact-valued correspondence (Debreu 1959).

We can now construct the correspondence $\bar{\Phi}$ from A: $S \times \Pi_{i=1}^n \mathscr{C}_R^i \times \Delta \times C$ into itself as follows.

$$(y^1, \ldots, y^n, z^1, \ldots, z^n) \xrightarrow{\lambda_\theta} \bar{\theta},$$

$$(\pi, \mu^i) \xrightarrow{\lambda_{a^i}} a^i, \qquad i = 1, \ldots, n,$$

$$(\mu^i, \bar{\theta}, \pi) \xrightarrow{\lambda^i} \mu^i, \qquad i = 1, \ldots, n,$$

$$(a^1, \ldots, a^n) \xrightarrow{\lambda_\pi} \pi, \qquad i = 1, \ldots, n.$$

Theorem 1.2. Under assumptions 1–3, 4.1 (for each consumer), and 5, there exists a long-run competitive equilibrium.

Proof. By Ascoli's theorem (Kelley, 1955, p. 233), $\mathscr{C}_R$ is compact. So A is a compact and convex set. Since $\bar{\Phi}$ is an uhc nonempty, convex, compact-valued correspondence, the Schauder-Tychonoff theorem (Dunford and Schwartz 1963) implies that it has a fixed point, which can be easily interpreted as a long-run competitive equilibrium.   QED

So far, we have obtained a long-run equilibrium in the following sense. If the auctioneer announces the equilibrium price vector at the beginning of each period, it will stay at the equilibrium price and consumers' expectations will be fulfilled. However, the stability properties of this type of long-run equilibrium may change over time; we may want a long-run equilibrium with invariant stability properties, that is, one for which the entire expectation function of every agent is stationary. Unfortunately, such an equilibrium is not possible because $\mathscr{C}$ is not compact. We can obtain such a result only by restricting the set of expectation functions to a convex compact subspace of $\mathscr{C}$. By Ascoli's theorem any convex closed equicontinuous subset will do.

We can use the technical apparatus developed in this section to show that the set of equilibrium prices and equilibrium actions behave continuously for continuous changes of expectations functions. This result is important if short-run equilibrium is to be a meaningful concept.

Let $\mathscr{E}$ be the short-run equilibrium correspondence from $\Pi_{i=1}^{n} \mathscr{C}^i$ into $S \times C$.

Theorem 1.3. $\mathscr{E}$ is an uhc, nonempty, compact, valued correspondence.

Proof. That $\mathscr{E}$ is nonempty follows from a classical Arrow-Debreu proof and the use of lemma 7. Consider a sequence of expectation functions Φ_j converging to Φ^* and a sequence of corresponding short-run equilibria $(\pi_j, a_j^1, \ldots, a_j^n)$ converging to $(\pi^*, a^{*1}, \ldots, a^{*n})$. Since $(a_j^1, \ldots, a_j^n)$ satisfies the feasibility conditions for each j, so does $(a^{*1}, \ldots, a^{*n})$. Since $\bar{\xi}^i(\pi, \Psi^i)$, the truncated action correspondence defined as a function of π and Ψ, is continuous for $i = 1, \ldots, n$, we have that $a_j^i \in \bar{\xi}^i(\pi_j, \Psi_j^i)$ implies $a^{*i} \in \bar{\xi}^i(\pi^*, \Psi^{*i})$ for $i = 1, \ldots, n$. We know that this fixed point $(\pi^*, a^{*1}, \ldots, a^{*n})$ is a short-run equilibrium (use the concavity of $U^i, i = 1, \ldots, n$). So $\mathscr{E}$ is a closed-graph correspondence; hence the result follows, since $S \times C$ is compact. QED

An Example

Consider an exchange economy with three goods and two markets. Good 1 is sold on its own market (market 1), but goods 2 and 3 are sold on the same market (market 2). Consumers are divided into two types of identical agents. There are equal numbers of each type, and the number is large, so competitive behavior is reasonable.

Let x_l^i be the consumption of good l ($l = 1, 2, 3$) by an agent of type i ($i = 1, 2$), and let w_l^i be the endowment of good l for an agent of type i. The price of good 1 is normalized to 1, and the price of melange (goods 2 and 3) is q.

Let $U^1(x_1^1, x_2^1, x_3^1) = x_1^1 + x_2^1$ be the utility function of any agent of type 1. His endowment consists of goods 2 and 3. His optimization program is then

$$\text{Max } x_1^1 + x_2^1$$

subject to

$$x_1^1 \leqq q(w_2^1 - x_2^1 + w_3^1 - x_3^1),$$
$$x_1^1 \geqq 0; \qquad w_2^1 \geqq x_2^1 \geqq 0; \qquad w_3^1 \geqq x_3^1 \geqq 0.$$

A typical consumer of type 2 owns only good 1 and cannot distinguish between goods 2 and 3 when he buys from market 2. Let $\bar{\theta}(q)$ be the market proportion of good 2 in the melange, when the price of melange is q. The proportion θ that the consumer obtains is a random variable with mean $\bar{\theta}(q)$. Let v be the quantity of melange he buys, and let $U^2(x_1^2, x_2^2, x_3^2) = x_1^2 + 2x_2^2$ be his utility function. Now x_2^2 is random, and the optimization problem of a consumer of type 2 is

$$\text{Max } E(x_1^2 + 2x_2^2)$$

subject to

$$x_2^2 = v\theta,$$
$$x_1^2 + qv \leqq w_1^2,$$
$$x_1^2 \geqq 0; \qquad x_2^2 \geqq 0; \qquad v \geqq 0$$

or

$$\text{Max } x_1^2 + 2vE\theta$$

subject to

$$x_1^2 + qv \leqq w_1^2,$$
$$x_1^2 \geqq 0,$$
$$v \geqq 0.$$

Instead of assuming that $E\theta$ is the true market proportion as a function of price, we postulate that agents of type 2 have an expected average proportion $\mu(q)$. Their demand correspondence is then

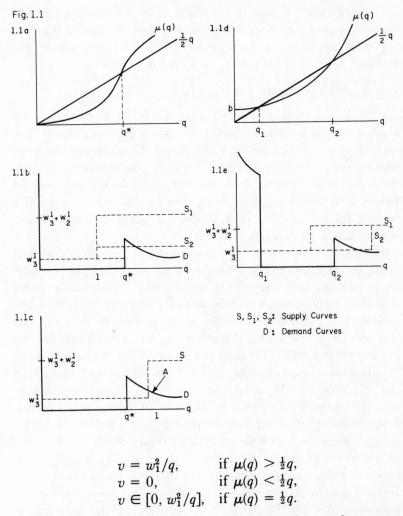

Fig. 1.1

S, S₁, S₂: Supply Curves
D : Demand Curves

$$v = w_1^2/q, \qquad \text{if } \mu(q) > \tfrac{1}{2}q,$$
$$v = 0, \qquad \text{if } \mu(q) < \tfrac{1}{2}q,$$
$$v \in [0, w_1^2/q], \quad \text{if } \mu(q) = \tfrac{1}{2}q.$$

Figure 1.1 shows different demand and supply correspondences and short-run equilibria. In figure 1.1b we have only one price equilibrium (with breakdown) when supply is S_1 or three equilibria when supply is S_2, depending on the relative values of w_2^1, w_3^1, w_1^2.

In figure 1.1d we have imposed assumption 4.2, in a crude way, by having $\mu(q)$ bounded below by b. At the associated equilibria there is no breakdown (figure 1.1e).

Now consider figure 1.1c. Point O is a long-run equilibrium, but point A may also be a long-run equilibrium. Take $(w_2^1 - w_3^1)/w_2^1 = k > \frac{1}{2}$ and $\mu(1) = k$. Then expectations are fulfilled at the equilibrium price vector $(1, 1)$.

Introducing Costly Information

Clearly incentives for structural changes exist in the economy. For example, buyers may want to determine the quality of goods before they buy them. To allow for this possibility, we introduce a special kind of costly information in the economic system. We use the same normalization of prices as in the second section; that is, the prices of good x belong to the simplex of R^L. Several interpretations of the model are then possible.

If we define a *unit of information* as the possibility of identifying in the market *one unit of good* y (resp. good z), then we may consider that each bit of information is sold by experts and that a consumer can hire experts to shop for him. Consumers pay for the time of the experts; that is, they pay for the cost of transmitting the information rather than for the information itself. This interpretation reduces the expert to an identification technology with fixed coefficients, which in the extreme can be a simple costly test or operation performed by the buyer himself. The technology of information is such that c_y (resp. c_z) units of each of the goods x are necessary to identify one unit of good y (resp. z). With only two goods in the melange we will have in general $c_y = c_z = c$, but this is not the case when there are three or more goods. Perfect competition is assumed in the production of information, so that if q is the price of one unit of melange, then $q_y = q + c_y$ and $q_z = q + c_z$ are the prices to consumers of good y and good z.

Let t^i (resp. s^i) be the quantity of good y (resp. z) purchased through experts. The optimization program of a consumer i is now

Max $V^i(x^i, y^i, z^i, t^i, s^i, v^i, \pi)$

$$= \int_{\Delta} u^i(x^i, y^i + t^i + \theta v^i, z^i + s^i + (1 - \theta)v^i)d\psi^i(\theta, \pi)$$

subject to

$$px^i + (q + c_y)t^i + (q + c_z)s^i + qv^i$$
$$\leq pw_x^i + q(w_y^i - y^i) + q(w_z^i - z^i),$$
$$x^i, y^i, z^i, t^i, s^i, v^i \geq 0; \qquad y^i \leq w_y^i; \qquad z^i \leq w_z^i.$$

Note that we do not allow for a sequential strategy in which a consumer first buys a quantity of melange and only then uses experts to obtain a desired proportion. When one of the goods is not desired, we obviously have $t^i s^i = 0$.

We could assume that the identification power bought from experts is not perfect. If η is the random success in the identification procedure, consumers will have subjective (or objective) probability distributions on this value, so the objective function can be written

$$\int_\Delta u^i(x^i, y^i + \eta t^i + (1 - \eta)s^i + \theta v^i, z^i + (1 - \eta)t^i$$
$$+ \eta s^i + (1 - \theta)v^i)d\Psi^i(\theta, \eta, \pi).$$

The problem is basically unchanged as long as experts are not identifiable. We therefore keep the previous formulation.

An *expertise short-run equilibrium* is a price system $(p^*, q^*) \in S \times R_+$ and a set of actions $(a^1, \ldots, a^n)$ that are solutions of the consumers' optimization programs such that

(i) $\sum_{i=1}^{n} (c_y s^i + c_z t^i) + \sum_{i=1}^{n} x^i \leq \sum_{i=1}^{n} w_x^i$

with $p \left[\sum_{i=1}^{n} (c_y s^i + c_z t^i) + x^i - w_x^i \right] = 0$;

(ii) $\sum_{i=1}^{n} (v^i + y^i + z^i + t^i + s^i) \leq \sum_{i=1}^{n} (w_y^i + w_z^i)$

with $q \left[\sum_{i=1}^{n} (v^i + y^i + z^i + t^i + s^i - w_y^i - w_z^i) \right] = 0$;

(iii) $\sum_{i=1}^{n} (t^i + y^i) \leq \sum_{i=1}^{n} w_y^i,$

$\sum_{i=1}^{n} (s^i + z^i) \leq \sum_{i=1}^{n} w_z^i.$

The *macroeconomic constraints* of condition (iii) express the idea that consumers should not find it impossible to use the information they can buy. In other words, at this stage we do not accept as an equilibrium a situation in which consumers can identify a good but cannot find it on the market. Clearly, then, in general there is no reason for this constraint to be satisfied. Let us construct such an example.

Consider again the example of the fourth section. The program of a buyer is now

$$\text{Max } x_1^2 + 2t + 2vE\theta(q)$$

subject to

$$x_1^2 + (q + c)t + qv \le w_1^2,$$
$$x_1^2, t, v \ge 0.$$

We take $0 < c < 1$ and a simple expectation function such

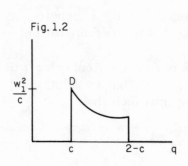

Fig. 1.2

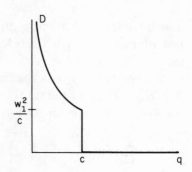

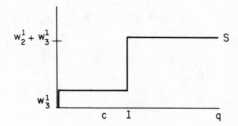

that $E\theta(q) = \frac{1}{2}$. We show now that no equilibrium exists if $c < w_1^2/w_3^1$. The supply and demand schedules are drawn in figure 1.2.

If $0 \leqq q < c$, demand for melange exceeds supply. If $q = c$, then a buyer's budget constraint becomes $2ct + cv = w_1^2$. Good y is not supplied at this price, so the only possibility is $t = 0$. Then $v = w_1^2/c$. But by assumption, $w_3^1 \neq w_1^2/c$. If $c < q < 1$, then there is no supply of good y but there is demand for it through experts. If $q \geqq 1$, then the demand for good y may fit if $w_1^2/(q + c) < w_2^1$. At this price sellers want to get rid of the remaining melange, but there is no demand for it.

Consequently when the price of expertise is low, there is no equilibrium. On the contrary, if $c > w_1^2/w_3^1$ there is an equilibrium at $q = w_1^2/w_3^1$. It appears that an expertise equilibrium may exist if the price of expertise is high enough.

We can offer two interpretations of how potential nonexistence can be overcome. Both involve identifying mechanisms (eventually not guided by prices) that will assure the macroeconomic constraints.

First, competition in the production of information introduces a fixed price-ratio, which is the source of nonexistence in our example. This fixed relationship can be broken by a monopolistic supplier of information; in terms of information the monopolist will be in charge of satisfying the macroeconomic constraints through his knowledge of demand conditions. It may also be possible to distort the price system with taxes in order to obtain an equilibrium. Let us compute such a tax in our example.

The budget constraint of a buyer is written

$$x_1^2 + rt + qv = w_1^2.$$

For $r = 2$ and $q = 1$, the supply of melange is less than or equal to $w_2^1 + w_3^1$. Equilibrium constraints are

$$t + v \leqq w_3^1 + w_2^1, \qquad t \leqq w_2^1,$$
$$v \geqq w_3^1, \qquad 2t + v = w_1^2.$$

If $w_1^2 \leqq w_2^1 + w_3^1$ and $w_3^1 \leqq w_2^1$, then an equilibrium exists for $v = w_3^1$ and $t = (w_1^2 - w_3^1)/2$, which is less than w_2^1. The appropriate tax is then given by $r = T + q + c$, or $T = 1 - c$. The purpose of taxation is not to reach an efficient point but more fundamentally to permit the economy to reach an equilibrium.

One way to satisfy the macroeconomic constraints is for consumers to be aware of them and to behave in a noncooperative way with respect to actions taken by others. Each consumer now has additional constraints:

$$t^i \leq \text{Max} \left(0, \sum_{i=1}^{n} w_y^i - \sum_{j=1; \, j \neq i}^{n} t^j \right),$$

$$s^i \leq \text{Max} \left(0, \sum_{i=1}^{n} w_z^i - \sum_{j=1; \, j \neq i}^{n} s^j \right).$$

Now it is easy to show the existence of a noncooperative equilibrium. We have a very special distribution of information, which allows for the fulfillment of the macroeconomic constraints, but note how important the distribution of information must be in this case. Other concepts of equilibrium could be introduced, such as equilibrim with rationing.

A second interpretation of the model is to regard experts as intermediaries who transform the melange into two different goods, labeled good y and good z. Let t^s (resp. s^s) be the supply of good y (resp. good z) by experts. For this production they use inputs of melange $t^d \geq 0$ (resp. $s^d \geq 0$) and inputs of goods $l = 1, \ldots, L$ represented by $x^y \geq 0$ and $x^z \geq 0$. Formally, we must have

$$t^s \leq \text{Min} \, (x_1^y/c_y, \, \ldots, \, x_L^y/c_y, \, t^d),$$
$$s^s \leq \text{Min} \, (x_1^z/c_z, \, \ldots, \, x_L^z/c_z, \, s^d).$$

There are two new markets for the products of experts and two associated prices q_y and q_z. Experts buy their inputs of good y and good z on the market for melange at a single price q and maximize profits. Here the macroeconomic constraints mean simply that the experts' demand for good y and good z should not exceed what is available on the market for melange.

$$t^d + \sum_i (y^i - w_y^i) \leqq 0$$

$$s^d + \sum_i (z^i - w_z^i) \leqq 0$$

Profit maximization implies

$$q_y \leqq q + c_y \quad \text{and} \quad q_z \leqq q + c_z,$$

with equality if experts are active. The definition of an equilibrium can be slightly modified in accordance with this interpretation, but modifications are minor.

The formalization of experts is satisfactory only if there is perfect competition in the production of information and if it costs nothing to find the right good once the consumer is able to identify the good. However, even when one can identify a good car, one must still find one, and this search cost goes to infinity as the proportion of good cars goes to zero. This search cost is in fact random, but for simplicity we will use a certainty equivalent approach.

Let c_y (resp. c_z) represent the identification cost plus the search cost to find good y (resp. z). The search cost clearly depends on the availability of good y in the market, so the following assumption is reasonable.

Assumption 6. Let $s_y = \sum_{i=1}^n (w_y^i - y^i)$ and $s_z = \sum_{i=1}^n (w_z^i - z^i)$. Then c_y is a positive continuous real function of s_y defined on $(0, \sum_{i=1}^n w_y^i]$, and $c_y(s_y)$ goes to infinity as s_y goes to zero. Similarly c_z is a positive continuous real function of s_z defined on $(0, \sum_{i=1}^n w_z^i]$, and $c_z(s_z)$ goes to infinity as s_z goes to zero.

Theorem 1.4. Assumptions 1–3, 4 (for one consumer), and 6, there exists an expertise short-run equilibrium (with a strictly positive price vector).

Proof. Let $\overline{R}_+$ be the compactified positive real line. (We adopt the convention $0 \times \infty = 0$.) Now c_y (resp. c_z) is considered a function from the compact convex set $[0, \Sigma_{i=1}^{n} w_y^i]$ (resp. $[0, \Sigma_{i=1}^{n} w_z^i]$) into $\bar{R}_+$. Consider the correspondence ζ from $S \times \bar{R}_+ \times \bar{R}_+$ into R^{L+1} defined as follows, with obvious notations.

$$\zeta(\pi, c_y, c_z) = \begin{cases} \displaystyle\sum_{i=1}^{n} [x^i(\pi, c_y, c_z) - w_x^i] \\[2mm] \displaystyle\sum_{i=1}^{n} [y^i(\pi, c_y, c_z) + z^i(\pi, c_y, c_z) + v^i(\pi, c_y, c_z) \\[2mm] \qquad + t^i(\pi, c_y, c_z) + s^i(\pi, c_y, c_z) - w_y^i - w_z^i] \end{cases}$$

Then a proof similar to that of theorem 1.1 can be obtained by juxtaposing to S the functions c_y and c_z in the fixed-point argument.   QED

This theorem allows equilibria with an infinite search cost. In appendix 1.B I construct such an example and give an assumption that eliminates this other form of breakdown for a market.

Efficiency

To deal meaningfully with efficiency in our model we have to compare alternative economic systems: a competitive economy with $L + 1$ markets and $L + 2$ goods, the same economy with experts, and eventually the same economy with costly supplementary markets. Recently Green and Sheshinski (1973) devised a methodology for comparing economic systems on the basis of efficiency.

An *economic system* is defined as a set of institutions, a choice of economic behaviors, and a concept of equilibrium; it may be summarized by the set of its equilibria. An economic system A is said to be efficient if there exists no other admissible economic system B such that an equilibrium of A is Pareto inferior to an equilibrium of B.

One interesting result given by this approach is that an equilibrium of an economy with some set of active institutions may be Pareto inferior to an equilibrium in an economy with a more restricted set of institutional possibilities. Green and Sheshinski show that in their model the necessary conditions for such an outcome are either nonconvexity of transaction costs or ownership patterns in which holdings of firms are highly concentrated. A similar example of *institutional inefficiency* for my model is not linked to the necessary conditions of Green and Sheshinski.

In the classical theory of value the largest feasible set is unambiguously defined by technological constraints. The main feature of my model is the dishonesty of sellers who do not reveal the quality of goods. It is unrealistic to consider reaching technological efficiency. However, if modifications of ethics (Arrow 1973; appendix 2.A) are allowed, a first-best problem would involve consideration of policies designed to encourage sellers to reveal the composition of the melange they sell. If extraeconomic penalties were available, one might attempt to force honest behavior by fear of high penalties, and we would then have to take into account the psychological and processing costs of such measures. Here we assume that we are constrained by the dishonesty of sellers.

Because of the remaining uncertainty, we cannot define allocations ex ante; we can only define imputations in terms of expected utility. It is appropriate to compare the ex ante imputations for the long-run equilibria in the different institutional frameworks, because expected imputations will correspond in the long run to average imputations.

In the following example an equilibrium of the economy with experts is Pareto inferior to the equilibrium of an economy without the institutional advantage of experts.

Consider again the long-run equilibrium A in figure 1.1c. If $(w_1^2 - w_3^1)/w_1^2 = k > \frac{1}{2}$ and $\mu(1) = k$, then expectations are fulfilled. If, further, $w_1^2 = w_2^1 + w_3^1$, then the ex ante imputations are

$$u_1 = w_2^1 + w_3^1,$$
$$u_2 = 2\mu(1)(w_2^1 + w_3^1) = 2k(w_2^1 + w_3^1).$$

Consider the economy with experts. The budget constraint of a type-2 consumer is

$$x_1^2 + (q + c)t + qv = w_1^2.$$

If $\mu(q) = q/(q + c)$, that is, if $\mu(1) = 1/(1 + c)$ for $q = 1$, then both good y and melange are bought.

Let $t \geq 0$ be such that

$$\frac{w_1^2 - (1 + c)t - w_3^1}{w_2^1 - (1 + c)t} = \frac{1}{1 + c}$$

or

$$t = \frac{w_1^2}{1 + c} - \frac{w_3^1}{c}$$

(which is possible for c large enough). Then

$$v = w_1^2 - (1 + c)t = \frac{1 + c}{c} w_3^1.$$

Therefore the imputations are

$$u_1 = w_2^1 + w_3^1,$$

$$u_2 = 2 \left(t + \frac{1}{1 + c} v \right) = 2 \frac{w_1^2}{1 + c}.$$

If we do not specify expectation functions in the definition of economic systems but simply say that the expectations of consumers must be fulfilled at the equilibrium, then if $c > (1 - k)/k$, the equilibrium with experts is Pareto inferior to the equilibrium without experts. The reason for this result is that the availability of experts leads to the direct purchase of good 2 so that expectations about the remaining melange must be scaled down to be fulfilled. Meanwhile resources have been employed to finance the expertise activity. The decentralized behavior of consumers induces the purchase of expertise and leads to this Pareto-inferior state. If consumers of type 2 colluded, they would reject the purchase of information and obtain a better state. This is an example of excessive purchase of information by competitive agents such as those suggested by Hirshleifer (1971). In our example without risk aversion, the long-run equilibrium without experts gives a maximum of Pareto-relevant information to consumers. In more general cases experts would decrease uncertainty with positive effects; thus the trade-off between risk aversion and information costs would be more complicated.

Conclusion

The presence of optimistic consumers prevents the market of melange from collapsing in the short run, even if adverse selection has this tendency in the long run. The existence of a long-run equilibrium leaves unanswered the question of existence of a revision of expectations which is reasonable, for example, from a Bayesian point of view and leads to a long-run equilibrium. In view of the negative results obtained by Arrow and Green (1973) and the complexity of uncertainty faced by consumers in this model, the matter should be cautiously explored with examples.

This chapter is a first attempt to study the consequences of making costly information available to consumers in a framework of *perfect competition,* that is, on the assumption that sellers and buyers are unidentifiable. The concept of information is not always meaningful without an associated concept of search cost.

However, it appears likely that making information available to buyers will encourage sellers to differentiate themselves. If such a differentiation is possible, then the competitive equilibrium might not be the right tool for analyzing this problem. A concept of monopolistic equilibrium is required to investigate advertising, guarantees, price quality policies, and so forth. Another approach might be to have a model in which the identifiability of sellers allows the coexistence of signaling and some form of competition. A game-theoretical approach is developed in the next chapter.

Appendix 1.A. Akerlof's Example

Consider an economy with two commodities; commodity 1, whose price is normalized to 1, is a usual good, and commodity 2 is a variable-quality good whose price is p. There are two types of agents, and the number of each is large enough to justify the competitive assumption.

A type-1 agent has a utility function

$$U^1 = x_1^1 + \int_0^{x_2^1} \mu(t)dt$$

where x_l^1, $l = 1, 2$, is the agent's consumption of good l and $\mu(\cdot)$ is the density function of the quality of good 2 consumed.

We assume that a type-1 agent owns N units of good 2 (his only initial resource), whose quality is uniformly distributed on $[0, 2]$. Because this agent is not identifiable, when he sells t units of good 2, he sells those units whose quality is between zero and $\mu(t) = 2t/N$, $t \in [0, N]$, and keeps the units with higher quality for his own consumption. His maximization program can then be written

$$\text{Max } x_1^1 + \int_{N-x_2^1}^{N} \mu(t)dt$$

subject to

$$x_1^1 = p(N - x_2^1).$$

He will therefore offer good 2 at any price up to $p = 2t/N$. His supply function for good 2 is then

$$\begin{aligned} Np/2, &\quad \text{if } p \le 2, \\ N, &\quad \text{if } p > 2. \end{aligned}$$

A type-2 agent has a utility function

$$U^2 = x_1^2 + \int_0^{x_2^2} \frac{3}{2} \mu(t)dt.$$

His initial resources are M units of good 1. Quality $\mu(t)$ is random for him, and we assume that he maximizes his expected utility. His maximization program is

$$\text{Max } E\left(x_1^2 + \int_0^{x_2^2} \frac{3}{2} \mu(t)dt\right)$$

subject to

$$x_1^2 + px_2^2 = M.$$

Since the agent is small, we can assume that $E\mu(t) = \mu$ for

Fig. 1.3

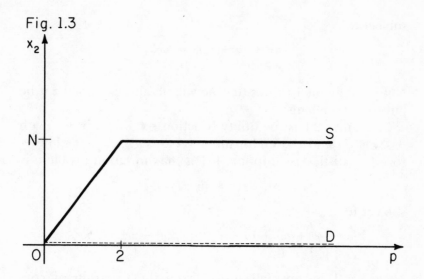

any $t \in [0, x_2^2]$. His demand correspondence for good 2 is then

$$
\begin{aligned}
x_2^2 &= M/p, && \text{if } 3\mu/2 > p, \\
x_2^2 &\in [0, M/p], && \text{if } 3\mu/2 = p, \\
x_2^2 &= 0, && \text{if } 3\mu/2 < p.
\end{aligned}
$$

Akerlof assumes that a type-2 agent knows the average quality of the supply of good 2 as a function of the price p, a rational expectation assumption. Here the average quality is

$$
\frac{1}{Np/2} \int_0^{Np/2} \frac{2t}{N} \, dt = \frac{p}{2}.
$$

Therefore for any p the demand of agent 2 is zero, leading to a breakdown of the market at a zero exchange level (figure 1.3).

Appendix 1.B.

Consider the following two-agent economy. Consumer 1 has the utility function $x^\alpha t^{1-\alpha}$, $\alpha > 0$, and the endowment w_x^1 of good x. His maximization problem is then

$$
\text{Max } x^\alpha \cdot t^{1-\alpha}
$$

subject to

$$px + (q + c_y)t = pw_x^1,$$
$$x \geqq 0; \quad t \geqq 0.$$

Note that agent 1 thinks that he will obtain only good z if he buys some melange.

Consumer 2 has the utility function $\epsilon(x + v) + y + t$ (with $0 < \epsilon < 1$) and the endowment vector (w_x^2, w_y^2, w_z^2). Therefore he satisfies assumption 4. His maximization problem is

$$\text{Max } \epsilon(x + v) + y + t$$

subject to

$$px + qy + qv + (q + c_y)t = q(w_z^2 + w_y^2) + pw_x^2,$$
$$x, y, v, t, \geqq 0.$$

Now $p = 1$ by normalization. From the program of consumer 2 it is clear that $q = 1$ is a possible equilibrium price. Then $y = w_y^2$, $x = w_x^2$, $v = w_z^2$ is a solution for consumer 2, so c_y goes to infinity and consumer 1 agonizes. However, the solution is an equilibrium.

We can make an assumption about the substitution between good x and good y (resp. good z) that guarantees more than the survival level to every consumer, even those without endowments in good y and good z.[4] Even though it looks complicated, this assumption is very simple and very weak.

Assumption 7.   There exists $K > 0$ such that for all $(x^i, y^i, t^i, s^i, z^i, \psi^i, \pi)$ the following are true.

     a. $t^i > 0$ implies the existence of x'^i such that

$$\int_\Delta u^i(x'^i, y^i + \theta v^i, z^i + s^i + (1 - \theta)v^i)d\psi^i(\theta, \pi)$$

$$> \int_\Delta u^i(x^i, y^i + t^i + \theta v^i, z^i + s^i + (1 - \theta)v^i)d\psi^i(\theta, \pi)$$

---

4. The survival level is defined as the minimum obtained by the utility function on the consumption set, which is R_+^{4+2} in this example.

and

$$\sum_{h=1}^{L} |x'^i_h - x^i_h| \le Kt_i.$$

b. $s^i > 0$ implies the existence of x''^i such that

$$\int_\Delta u^i(x''^i, y^i + t^i + \theta v^i, z^i + (1 - \theta)v^i)d\psi^i(\theta, \pi)$$

$$> \int_\Delta u^i(x^i, y^i + t^i + \theta v^i, z^i + s^i + (1 - \theta)v^i)d\psi^i(\theta, \pi)$$

and

$$\sum_{h=1}^{L} |x''^i_h - x^i_h| \le Ks^i.$$

Theorem 1.5. Under assumptions 1–3, 4 for one consumer, 6, and 7 there exists an expertise short-run equilibrium (with a strictly positive price vector) such that no consumer is at the survival level.

Proof. From assumption 7 it is clear that when $c_y > K$ (or $c_z > K$) no information for good y (good z) is purchased. Suppose that $t^i > 0$, and take x'^i as defined in assumption 7. Then from the price normalization we have

$$px'^i - px^i \le \sum_{h=1}^{L} |x'^i_h - x^i_h| < Kt^i.$$

Therefore $(x'^i, y^i, 0, s^i, z^i)$ is preferred to $(x^i, y^i, t^i, s^i, z^i)$ and is feasible, a contradiction.

Now let $\overline{K}$ denote the interval $[0, K]$, and let ξ_y, ξ_z be functions from R^n_+ into $\overline{K}$ defined as follows.

$$\xi_y: (y^1, \ldots, y^n) \to \tilde{c}_y = \text{Min} \left[c_y \left(\sum_{i=1}^{n} (w^i_y - y^i) \right), K \right]$$

$$\xi_z: (z^1, \ldots, z^n) \to \tilde{c}_z = \text{Min} \left[c_z \left(\sum_{i=1}^{n} (w^i_z - z^i) \right), K \right]$$

Consider the correspondence ζ from $S \times \overline{K} \times \overline{K}$ into R^{L+1} defined as follows, with obvious notations.

$$
\zeta(\pi, \tilde{c}_y, \tilde{c}_z) \begin{cases} \displaystyle\sum_{i=1}^{n} (x^i(\pi, \tilde{c}_y, \tilde{c}_z) - w_x^i) \\[2ex] = \displaystyle\sum_{i=1}^{n} [y^i(\pi, \tilde{c}_y, \tilde{c}_z) + z^i(\pi, \tilde{c}_y, \tilde{c}_z) + v^i(\pi, \tilde{c}_y, \tilde{c}_z) \\[2ex] \qquad + t^i(\pi, \tilde{c}_y, \tilde{c}_z) + s^i(\pi, \tilde{c}_y, \tilde{c}_z) - w_y^i - w_z^i] \end{cases}
$$

Using the fact that $\tilde{c}_y$ and $\tilde{c}_z$ belong to a compact set, we can obtain a proof similar to the proof of theorem 1.1 by juxtaposing the functions ξ_y and ξ_z to ξ in the fixed-point argument. Clearly the price system and the search costs are such that no consumer can be at his survival level.   QED

2

Core with Asymmetrical Information

The concept of core has been used in economics to define a set of socially stable outcomes. Under convexity assumptions the core of an exchange economy is nonempty (Scarf 1967). Moreover, the competitive equilibrium, when it exists, belongs to the core. These results have been generalized to ϵ-cores and ϵ-equilibria when convexity does not hold but the number of agents is large (Shapley and Shubik 1966; Arrow and Hahn 1971; Hildenbrand, Schmeidler, Zamir 1971). Debreu and Scarf (1963) showed that the core is equitable, in the sense of giving similar endowments to similar agents. This result was criticized by Green (1972) and generalized by Hildenbrand and Kirman (1973). The most important result was that with a large number of agents the core shrinks to the set of equilibria. This result was first obtained by Edgeworth (1881) and was made rigorous by Debreu and Scarf (1963), Hildenbrand (1974), Aumann (1964), Bewley (1973), Arrow and Hahn (1971), and Brown and Robinson (1972).

The use of the core in economics has often been criticized on the ground that it requires enormous flows of information. All possible coalitions must be considered before one can be sure that an imputation belongs to the core. Some attempts have been made to limit the number of coalitions (Luce and Raiffa 1957), but they have not been convincing because their limitations are not based on any reasonable theory of information.

The theory of the core may be adapted to deal with an economy with a basic informational constraint by limiting, not the number of coalitions, but their power.

A Game Theory Approach

Equilibrium analysis gives several insights into the nature of the problem but also reveals a tendency toward less impersonal relations between consumers. One tempting approach is to introduce possible cooperative behaviors. One concept of game theory, the core, may be used for such an analysis.

The framework is the same as in chapter 1. We replace assumptions 3 and 4 by the following assumption.

Assumption 8. The endowments are such that $w_x^i > 0$, $w_y^i + w_z^i > 0$, $i = 1, \ldots, n$, and the utility function u^i is strictly increasing in each argument, $i = 1, \ldots, n$.

Trade can take place through bargaining without a price system. Our main interest is in defining and studying such bargaining in the economy where informational constraints have to be taken into account. Let us first assume that expectations ψ^i are independent of v^i, $i = 1, \ldots, n$.

To define an optimum, we assume as in Diamond (1967) that the center has the same informational constraints as the market.

An imputation $(u^{*1}, \ldots, u^{*n})$ is feasible if there exist actions (a^i), $i = 1, \ldots, n$. such that

$$\sum_{i=1}^{n} x^i \leq \sum_{i=1}^{n} w_x^i; \tag{2.1}$$

$$\sum_{i=1}^{n} (v^i + y^i + z^i) \leq \sum_{i=1}^{n} (w_y^i + w_z^i); \tag{2.2}$$

$$y^i \leqq w_y^i, \qquad i = 1, \ldots, n;$$
$$z^i \leqq w_z^i, \qquad i = 1, \ldots, n; \tag{2.3}$$

$$x^i, y^i, z^i, v^i \geqq 0; \tag{2.4}$$

$$\int_\Delta u^i(x^i, y^i + \theta v^i, z^i + (1 - \theta)v^i)d\psi^i(\theta) = u^{*i}$$
$$i = 1, \ldots, n. \tag{2.5}$$

Definition. An imputation $(u^{*1}, \ldots, u^{*n})$ is an *informationally restricted optimum* if there exist no actions (a^i), $i = 1, \ldots, n$, such that (1) they are feasible and (2) $U^i(x^i, y^i, z^i, v^i) > u^{*i}$, $i = 1, \ldots, n$.

The strict inequality for each agent is equivalent to the inequality $\geq$ for each $i = 1, \ldots, n$, with at least one strict inequality because of the strict monotonicity of preferences. The concept of optimum now depends on the distribution of initial endowments.

We impose in this definition the same informational constraints as in the market, because we do not allow the center to distribute quantities of true goods y and z larger than initial endowments. Agents do not expect more from the center than from the market.

We define the core of the economy in the same way. We assume that in a coalition C an agent is never sure of having goods y and z in quantities larger than his own resources. Moreover, we assume that expectations about the proportion of good y *do not vary with coalitions.*

A coalition C is a subset of the set of agents $N = \{1, \ldots, n\}$. A coalition C blocks an imputation $(u^{*1}, \ldots, u^{*n})$ if there exist actions (a^i), $i = 1, \ldots, n$, such that

$$\sum_{i \in C} x^i \leqq \sum_{i \in C} w_x^i,$$

$$\sum_{i \in C} (v^i + y^i + z^i) \leqq \sum_{i \in C} (w_y^i + w_z^i),$$

$$y^i \leqq w_y^i,$$
$$z^i \leqq w_z^i,$$
$$x^i, y^i, z^i, v^i \geqq 0 \quad \text{for each } i \in C, \tag{2.6}$$

and

$$U^i(x^i, y^i, z^i, v^i) = \int_\Delta u^i(x^i, y^i + \theta v^i, z^i + (1 - \theta)v^i)d\psi^i(\theta)$$
$$> u^{*i}, \quad i \in C. \quad (2.7)$$

The core is the set of feasible imputations that are not blocked by any coalition. The set of feasible imputations would be different without the informational constraint. The coalitions are also constrained by the "dishonesty" of traders, so their power is limited relative to that of coalitions without the informational constraint.

Properties of Informationally Constrained Cores

We ask three questions. Is the core nonempty? Is it equitable? What are the relations between the core and the equilibrium defined in chapter 1?

Let us normalize utility functions such that $u^i(w_x^i, w_y^i, w_z^i) = 0$. Let V_C be the set of imputations that coalition C can realize. We restrict V_C to the set of imputation vectors with positive components. With the assumption of free disposal, V_C is clearly compact, and if $u \in V_C$ and $u' \in R_+^{|C|}$ with $u' \leq u$, then $u' \in V_C$.

Proposition 2.1. The core is nonempty under assumptions 2–8.

Proof. According to Scarf's theorem (1967), it is sufficient to show that the associated game is balanced. Let T be a balanced collection of coalitions (there exist positive weights $\delta_C > 0$ with $\Sigma_{C \in T, C \supset \{i\}} \delta_C = 1$ for all $i = 1, \ldots, n$), and let u be a vector of imputations such that $u_C \in V_C$ for all $C \in T$. We must show that $u \in V_N$. Since $u_C \in V_C$, there exist $(x_C^i, y_C^i, z_C^i, v_C^i)$, $i = 1, \ldots, n$, such that

$$\sum_{i \in C} (x_C^i - w_C^i) \leq 0;$$

$$\sum_{i \in C} (v_C^i + y_C^i + z_C^i - w_y^i - w_z^i) \leq 0;$$

$x_C^i, y_C^i, z_C^i, v_C^i \geqq 0; \quad y_C^i \leqq w_y^i; \quad z_C^i \leqq w_z^i \quad \text{for all } i \in C;$

$U^i(x_C^i, y_C^i, z_C^i, v_C^i)$

$$= \int_\Delta u^i(x_C^i, y_C^i + \theta v_C^i, z_C^i + (1 - \theta)v_C^i)d\psi^i(\theta)$$

$$= u_C^i \quad \text{for all } i \in C.$$

Consider $(x^i, y^i, z^i, v^i) = \Sigma_{C \in T, C \supset \{i\}}\delta_C(x_C^i, y_C^i, z_C^i, v_C^i),$ the convex combination of allocations obtained in the different coalitions, with the weights used in the definition of balanced coalitions.

By concavity of u^i we have

$U^i(x^i, y^i, z^i, v^i) \geqq u^i \quad \text{for all } C \in T, C \supset \{i\}, i = 1, \ldots, n.$

Therefore if (x^i, y^i, z^i, v^i) is feasible, u belongs to V_N and the game is balanced. It is indeed feasible.

$$\sum_{i=1}^n x^i = \sum_{i=1}^n \sum_{\substack{C \supset \{i\} \\ C \in T}} \delta_C x_C^i = \sum_{C \in T} \delta_C \sum_{i \in C} x_C^i \leqq \sum_{C \in T} \delta_C \sum_{i \in C} w_x^i$$

$$= \sum_{i=1}^n w_x^i \sum_{C \in T, C \supset \{i\}} \delta_C = \sum_{i=1}^n w_x^i.$$

Similarly we can show that $\Sigma_{i=1}^n(v^i + y^i + z^i) \leqq \Sigma_{i=1}^n(w_y^i + w_z^i).$ Since we take a convex combination, we have that $y^i \leqq w_y^i,$ $z^i \leqq w_z^i,$ and $x^i, y^i, z^i, v^i \geqq 0$ for $i = 1, \ldots, n.$ QED

Proposition 2.2.   If the Von Neumann utility functions u^i are strictly concave, $i = 1, \ldots, n,$ then the core is equitable.

Proof.   Consider an economy with I types of agents with r individuals in each type. Let $(x^{iq}, y^{iq}, z^{iq}, v^{iq}), i = 1, \ldots, I,$ $q = 1, \ldots, r,$ be an allocation in the core for which agents of the same type do not have the same bundle of goods.

Different bundles cannot provide the same level of utility for agents of the same type because of strict concavity. Then consider a coalition C formed with the worst-off agent of each type. The feasibility of $(x^{iq}, y^{iq}, z^{iq}, v^{iq}), i = 1, \ldots, I,$

$q = 1, \ldots, r$, for the whole economy implies the feasibility of the following allocation for coalition C.

$$\left(\frac{1}{r} \sum_{q=1}^{r} x^{iq}, \frac{1}{r} \sum_{q=1}^{r} y^{iq}, \frac{1}{r} \sum_{q=1}^{r} z^{iq}, \frac{1}{r} \sum_{q=1}^{r} v^{iq} \right).$$

By strict concavity of the utility function, coalition C can then block the initial allocation.   QED

Proposition 2.3.   The short-run competitive equilibrium is in the core.

Proof.   Suppose that the allocation (x^i, y^i, z^i, v^i), $i = 1, \ldots, n$, of the short-run competitive equilibrium is blocked by a coalition C. Then there exists (x'^i, y'^i, z'^i, v'^i), $i \in C$, feasible for C, such that

$$U^i(x'^i, y'^i, z'^i, v'^i) > U^i(x^i, y^i, z^i, v^i) \quad \text{for each } i \in C.$$

The definition of the short-run equilibrium implies

$$px'^i + q(y'^i + z'^i + v'^i) > pw_x^i + q(w_y^i + w_z^i), \quad i \in C.$$

Then summing over i we get a contradiction of the feasibility constraint.   QED

These propositions are similar to classical ones. However, two important results were not obtained. First, the proposition that an equilibrium with transfers corresponds to each optimum has no meaning here, since the concept *optimum* depends on the initial allocation of endowments. Second, it does not appear possible to show directly that the core shrinks to the set of equilibria when the number of agents increases to infinity.

An Example

Consider an economy with two consumers and three goods (x, y, z). Consumer 1 has an endowment vector $w^1 = (0, \frac{1}{2}, \frac{1}{2})$. His utility function is $x_1^1 + x_2^1$ (where x_j^i is consumption of good j by consumer i). Consumer 2 has an endowment vector $w^2 = (1, 0, 0)$. His utility function is $x_1^2 + 2x_2^2$.

There is an asymmetry of information in the sense that

agent 2 in his bargain with agent 1 cannot distinguish ex ante good y from good z. Hence the utility function of agent 2 may be rewritten $x_1^2 + 2v^2 E\theta$ where v^2 is the total quantity of goods y and z that agent 2 consumes, and $E\theta$ is the expected proportion of good y in this quantity. In order to represent both utility functions in the same space, we may rewrite the utility function of agent 1 as $x_1^1 + v^1 E\theta$, where $E\theta = 1$ for $0 \leqq v^1 \leqq \frac{1}{2}$ and $E\theta = 1/2v^1$ for $v^1 > \frac{1}{2}$. We represent the economy in an Edgeworth box and choose different values of the expectation functions (figure 2.1).

The introduction of the quantity of melange v in expectations leads in general to nonconvexities that destroy all the

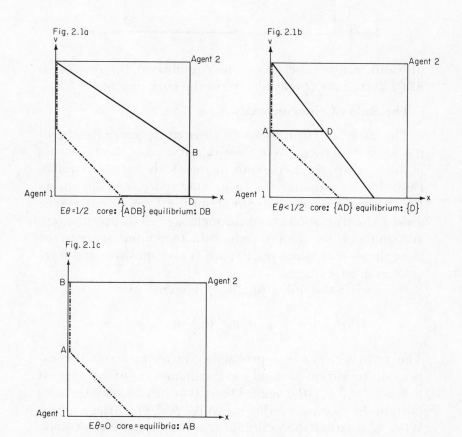

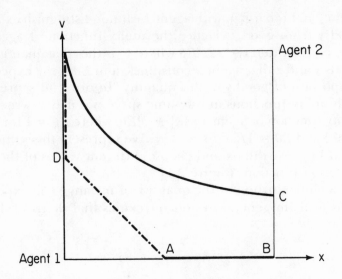

previous results. There exists no equilibrium, but the core is *ABC*. Eventually *D* may also be in the core (see figure 2.2).

The Role of Nonconvexity

The proof of Debreu-Scarf's theorem requires the use of the separation theorem to show that if an allocation is always in the core when the economy increases, then it is an equilibrium. In our economy the bargaining space is of dimension $L + 3$; that is, agents bargain about the L goods x, the true good y, the true good z, and the melange v. To apply the separation theorem, we must reduce the bargaining space to the same dimension as the price space. This is possible, but it reveals nonconvexities.

We rewrite the utility function of agent i as

$$U^i(x^i, v^i) = \int_\Delta u^i(x^i, \theta v^i, (1 - \theta)v^i)d\psi^i(v^i, \theta).$$

The term $\psi^i(v^i, \theta)$ is a probability measure about the expected proportion of good y in the quantity v^i of melange. If $v^i \leqq \min(w^i_y, w^i_x)$, the agent knows that he can keep the proportion he wants, so the measure $\psi(v^i, \theta)$ is degenerate. When v^i is larger than $\min(w^i_y, w^i_x)$, the measure is a combination of what he can obtain from his own endowments and what he expects to obtain in bargaining. Then $U^i(x^i, v^i)$ is nonconcave, so we cannot apply the Debreu-Scarf result.

In other words, the device that extends the choice space and thus enables us to analyze the problem with classical tools was a means of suppressing a nonconvexity in the reduced space. An analysis using the concepts of ϵ-equilibria and ϵ-cores is then necessary.

More Consistent Expectations

So far we have shown that a certain type of expectation allows an analysis of our problem quite similar to the classical analysis. In this approach expectations in bargaining are taken to be independent of coalitions and identical to expectations formed in a market situation.

A more general theory involves expectations that depend on coalitions. Then the model changes dramatically. There are multiple ways of constructing consistent expectations. To simplify our classification of these constructions, we assume that good z is of no use to any consumer.

GAME 1

Each agent has prior beliefs about the endowments of each other agent $\psi^i(j)$. When a coalition is realized, all agents put their endowments of goods y and z in a pool, and the allocations of melange are drawn from the pool. Agents are therefore able to construct an expectation measure about the proportion of good y in the pool.

We say that a coalition C realizes the imputation (u^{*i}), $i \in C$, if there exist (x^i, v^i), $i \in C$, such that

$$\sum_{i \in C} (x^i - w_x^i) \leqq 0,$$

$$\sum_{i \in C} (v^i - w_m^i) \leqq 0 \quad \text{with } w_m^i = w_y^i + w_z^i, \, i \in C,$$

$$x^i, v^i \geqq 0, \qquad i \in C,$$

$$\int_\Delta u^i(x^i, \theta v^i, (1 - \theta)v^i)d\psi^i(\theta, C) = u^{*i}, \qquad i \in C,$$

$$\psi^i(\theta, C) = F^1((w_m^j), \psi^i(j), j \in C, j \neq i),$$

where F^1 is the operator that constructs the expectation measure from initial beliefs.

GAME 2

Agents put into the pool only the quantities of goods y and z that they do not keep. Each agent knows the global quantity $(y^j + z^j)$ kept by each other agent j of the coalition. He is therefore able to construct an expectation measure about the differences $\bar{w}_m^j = (w_m^j - y^j - z^j)$ which are put into the pool from which he draws his allocation of melange. This expectation measure and therefore the utility function now depend on the action $(y^j + z^j)$ taken by all the other agents in the coalition. We then introduce difficulties reminiscent of the definition of the core with externalities (Shapley and Shubik 1969, Starrett 1973b).

A coalition C can realize the imputation (u^{*i}), $i \in C$, if there exist (x^i, y^i, z^i, v^i), $i \in C$, such that

$$\sum_{i \in C} (x^i - w_x^i) \leq 0,$$
$$\sum_{i \in C} (v^i + y^i + z^i - w_y^i - w_z^i) \leq 0,$$
$$x^i, y^i, z^i, v^i \geq 0, \qquad y^i \leq w_y^i, \qquad z^i \leq w_z^i, \qquad i \in C,$$
$$\int_\Delta u^i(x^i, y^i + \theta v^i, z^i + (1 - \theta)v^i) d\psi^i(\theta, (y^j + z^j),$$
$$j \in C, j \neq i) = u^{*i}, \qquad i \in C,$$
$$\psi^i(\cdot) = F^2(w_m^j, \psi^i(j), (y^j + z^j), j \in C, j \neq i).$$

In games 1 and 2 the use of the pool is crucial to destroy the superadditivity of the game. When a coalition is created, individual relationships lose their relevance, and opportunities for advantageous exchanges disappear because of the averaging effect of the equation defining expectations. The use of the pool is also crucial in simplifying the structure of the model.

GAME 3

In the absence of a pool we must not only introduce pairwise exchanges but also record the order of these exchanges, since the amount of melange varies with the agent's rank in the exchange process (we assume that an agent gives first what he likes the least). In the definition of a feasible imputation for a coalition, the expectation measure is a complicated function of the allocations of other consumers.

The information necessary for such a game may be available when the number of players is very small, but it is not available in games involving a large number of players. We must expect this information to be only very imperfectly distributed; to each such distribution corresponds a concept of core.

These are only a few of the examples that show how crucially the core depends on the information available to agents.

We can obtain a general result if we are willing to make assumptions about expected utility functions.

Assumption 9. Expectations are such that for each coalition $C \subset N$ and for all (x^i, y^i, z^i, v^i), all $i \in N$,

$$\int_\Delta u^i(x^i, y^i + \theta v^i, z^i + (1 - \theta)v^i)d\psi^i(\theta, C)$$
$$\leqq \int_\Delta u^i(x^i, y^i + \theta v^i, z^i + (1 - \theta)v^i)d\psi^i(\theta, N).$$

This assumption, with concavity, assures that the game is balanced.

Proposition 2.4. Under assumptions 1–4 the core is not empty.

The proof is left to the reader.

The lack of superadditivity in our problem suggests the relevance of a concept slightly different from the core. For example, we could say that an imputation $(u^1, \ldots, u^n)$ is feasible for the economy if there exists a partition $(N_1, \ldots, N_L)$ of N such that each coalition N_k can realize the imputation (u^i), $i \in N_k$, $k = 1, \ldots, L$.

Empty Core with Variable Expectations

Consider an economy with three consumers and three goods. All consumers have the same endowment vector, namely, $(1, \frac{1}{2}, \frac{1}{2})$. They all have the same utility function

$$x_1^i + x_2^i + v^i \theta^i(C), \qquad i = 1, 2, 3,$$

where x_j^i is the consumption of good j by consumer i, v^i is the quantity of melange obtained by consumer i, and $\theta^i(C)$ is his expectation about the proportion of good 2 in the melange when he belongs to coalition C. These expectations are constructed from the following initial beliefs. Consumer 1 expects consumer 2 to have one unit of good 2 (zero of good 3), consumer 3 to have no units of good 2 (one of good 3), and similarly for other consumers by circular permutation.

The crucial point is, How is $\theta^i(C)$ defined? From his information, consumer i expects given quantities of good 2 and 3 to be in the hands of his partners in coalition C. What proportion of good 2 may he expect from a quantity of melange that he obtains? Several possibilities exist.

He may be very pessimistic and think that he will first obtain good 3. Only if he gets more than the total quantity of good 3 in the coalition will he expect to obtain some of good 2. Then coalition $(1, 2)$ can realize the imputation $(1.5 + x, 2 - x)$ for $0 \leq x \leq 0.5$ as follows. Consumer 1 gets one unit of melange from consumer 2 (value 1) plus his endowment of good 2, that is, $1 + 0.5 = 1.5$. Then good 1 is shared to give the announced imputation. By permutation, coalitions $(2, 3)$ and $(3, 1)$ can realize the same.

Now consider coalition $(1, 2, 3)$. The only individually rational imputation is $(1.5, 1.5, 1.5)$, which can be realized in different ways. (1) Everyone keeps his initial endowment. (2) Two units of melange are given to agent 1 (value 1) plus his endowment of good 2 (1.5). The three units of good 1 are shared by agents 2 and 3. (3) The same as (2), by permutation.

Up to one unit of melange, the agent expects to get only good 3. In this case the core is empty and there is no undominated imputation. If we allow coalition (1, 2, 3) to be split into subcoalitions to get its best imputation we obtain

$$(1.5, 1.5 + x, 2 - x)$$

or

$$(2 - x, 1.5, 1.5 + x)$$

or

$$(1.5 + x, 2 - x, 1.5).$$

The core is still empty. This is an illustration of Gillies's result (1959) that any game is equivalent to a superadditive game whose characteristic function v' is obtained from the characteristic function v of the initial game by

$$v'(C) = \text{Max} \sum_G v(C_i),$$

where the sum is over all partitions of C. This is exactly what we did when we allowed the coalition (1, 2, 3) to be split up. (Gillies's result is valid for games with transferable utilities, but this is in fact what we have through good 1.)

This pessimistic approach is consistent with traditional game theory, but it does not seem very satisfactory in our context. Another possibility is to allow several channels of exchange in coalition (1, 2, 3). Agent 2 gives his melange to agent 1, agent 3 gives his to agent 2, agent 1 gives his to agent 3. Then the imputation (2, 2, 2) is realized and the core is not empty. But if so many communication channels are created, then why would they not exchange information? The question then is, Do the pessimistic convince the optimistic (and then we are back to (1.5, 1.5, 1.5)), or do the optimistic convince the pessimistic (and then (2, 2, 2) can be realized in many ways)?

Another possibility is not to allow personal exchanges once a coalition is formed but to allow for less pessimistic expectations. The extreme optimistic position, in which consumers expect first to get good 2, would lead to the following. As before, coalition (1, 2) obtains $(1.5 + x, 2 - x)$, but coalition (1,

2, 3) can realize (2, 2, 2). But this is even less reasonable than the pessimistic position, since agents give away their good 3 and expect to get good 2.

Intermediate situations are more difficult to make precise because they depend on how much more information we are willing to give to consumers. If a consumer knows the actions taken by other consumers of the coalition with respect to their holdings (how much they kept of each endowment), they may have a better idea of what is available in the melange. But then the situation becomes really complicated.

There is another possibility. From the global quantities in the hands of their partners they compute a proportion of good 2, and they expect to obtain this proportion. Then coalition (1, 2, 3) obtains (1.5, 1.5, 1.5) or (1.7, 1.7, 1.7), depending on whether they throw their endowments into the pool of melange. In either case the core is empty.

This chapter has done little more than illustrate the difficulty of studying cooperative behavior in games with imperfect information. The study of cooperative games with differential information clearly awaits further work. (See appendix 2.A for a different approach.)

Appendix 2.A. Macroeconomic Constraints, Economic Efficiency, and Ethics

The purpose of this appendix is to ask questions about the realism, the implications, and the possible modifications of the usual formalizations of the behavior of economic agents when they are very numerous and are subjected to macroeconomic constraints.[1] The common practice is to assume self-

---

1. A first draft of this appendix was slightly revised after reading Arrow's paper (1973). Arrow sees two main reasons for introducing ethics considerations, pollution, and disequilibria in information endowments. He conducts his argument for firms. Part of this appendix may be viewed as a special case of Arrow's. It focuses on consumers instead of firms and investigates the consequences of Kantian ethics. This appendix deals essentially with externality problems and some macroeconomic constraints not usually viewed as externalities.

ish behavior, which is viewed as an unalterable fact of social and economic life. The relevance of large numbers in our problem is that the consequences for the community of individual actions may be of a much larger order of magnitude than that for individuals themselves. Theories of cooperative behavior that go beyond selfish individual interest have been proposed for cases in which the number of agents is small, but in the present context they are too complex or too costly in terms of information.

The phenomena that I wish to propose are the possibility and the consequences of collective behavior (without any direct communication between agents), in contradiction to the maximization of direct personal interest. Such behavior may be induced by making people aware of a macroeconomic constraint. The state may play a major role in the realization of conditions favorable to the awakening of this consciousness.

The basic assumption is that human nature in some economic circumstances is capable of behavior other than the selfish pattern imputed to it by economic theory. I shall show by examples that such behavior has been revealed in past events. That unselfish behavior is possible implies that it may be optimal when one is choosing among possible policies to induce such behavior (by the diffusion of the appropriate information, for example). I do not mean to imply that most problems can be solved this way. "One must not expect miraculous transformations in human behaviour. Ethical codes, if they are viable, should be limited in scope" (Arrow 1973, p. 316).

To give substance to the concept of a new ethics, I postulate that a typical agent assumes (according to Kant's moral) that the other agents will act as he does and that he maximizes his utility function under this new constraint. When behavior is noncooperative, agents suppose that the others will continue to act as they do at the decision date. My proposition is then equivalent to a special assumption about the anticipation of others' reaction functions. Clearly the meaning of "the same action" depends on the model and

usually means "the same *kind* of action." However, to simplify the argument we choose economies with identical
agents so that it is literally true. My purpose is to illustrate an
idea rather than to present a complete model.

The argument consists of essentially two points. First, inducing people to behave in a Kantian way may be a very
good solution to some problems, and the relevance of such a
policy is related to the existence of macroeconomic constraints. Second, knowing whether people take into account
macroeconomic constraints is an important clue to understanding many different problems.

Looking for Unselfish Behavior

Let us consider the case of a large homogeneous beach
where a large number of anonymous people come every day.
Garbage cans are located every one hundred meters. The
impact on the individual's welfare of throwing his own beer
cans on the beach is negligible by assumption, and it is tiring
to reach a garbage can. But the agent's welfare depends on
the total number of beer cans scattered over the beach. How
is it possible that (at least in some countries) people do not
leave their beer cans on the beaches? A classical argument
may rest on the hope that a demonstration effect will work.
However, with anonymous people the strength of this argument can easily be weakened. What is the best way to describe the decision process of these people?

Every economic action takes place in the framework of a
moral or ethic. The moral based on the main rules "do not
injure your neighbor's person or his property" and "have
freely entered but binding contracts on markets" appears to
have worked well until recently, at least as far as economic efficiency was concerned. Modern times reveal increasing economic interdependences that are not marketable (because of
physical impossibility or excessive cost). The possibility of
changing the ethic or of modifying the social responsibilities
of citizens must be investigated. The beach example shows
that in some countries citizens have appreciated their new
responsibilities, and I argue that Kant's rule fits the framework of their new decision process.

Other examples come to mind. In the United States taxation or rationing to solve the energy problem is considered very costly, and the government instead asks Americans to voluntarily conserve energy. Why should this approach work if people are selfish maximizers? The demonstration effect cannot even be invoked here. Something else is expected of Americans. It is reasonable to expect a kind of Kantian behavior in this case and to expect that this approach will work if the operation is conducted well. Providing information through the news media is inexpensive, which is yet another argument for this solution. The government hopes that people will become aware of the relevant macroeconomic constraint and adopt Kantian behavior under this constraint.

The stability of this type of solution creates the same problems (even more acutely) as the stability of cooperative solutions. But the problems that are created are not much different from the problems of enforcing the civil code. Ethical and social pressures must be combined to keep the number of cheaters negligible.

People have already shown their ability to go beyond selfish maximization. Most beaches and highways are not littered to the extent suggested by selfish behavior. This being the case, we must ask how we can analyze such behavior economically.

THE SUFFICIENCY OF SELFISH BEHAVIOR

We repeat in this section the well-known efficiency property of market economies with individual maximizers and the uselessness of Kantian behavior in this framework. We assume that all agents have the same (differentiable, increasing, and concave) utility function. The conceptualization of *large number* is borrowed from Aumann (1964), and we use a measurable space of agents $A = [0, 1]$ endowed with the Lebesgue measure μ. There are two commodities x and y in this economy; the initial endowments are $(1, 1)$ for each agent. We normalize the price of x to 1. It is possible to transform good x into good y according to the process $y \leqq \alpha x$. The price of good y is then usually $p = 1/\alpha$.

The optimization problem of a consumer is then

$$\text{Max } U(x, y)$$

subject to

$$x + (1/\alpha)y = 1 + (1/\alpha)1,$$

which gives $U_2/U_1 = 1/\alpha$ (if we assume, as we will through-out this appendix, that we have interior solutions).

The only macroeconomic constraints of this model are essentially additive constraints on resources.

$$\int_A x d\mu = 1 \quad \text{and} \quad \int_A y d\mu = 1$$

The special characteristic of these constraints is that considering only the equilibrium price $p = 1/\alpha$ allows agents to behave in a way that is consistent with these constraints and Pareto optimal. In this framework it is fruitless in terms of economic efficiency for consumers to behave unselfishly. The only consequence of Kantian behavior would be the immediate realization of the equilibrium without any tâton-nement process. In more general models this result would not hold without a better definition of "the same kind of behavior" and without requiring a great deal of information. The sufficiency of selfish behavior for efficiency in this case has led many economists to accept without question the behavioral assumption of individual maximization.

CONSUMPTION EXTERNALITIES AND SOCIAL RESPONSIBILITY

We modify slightly the example of the preceding section to introduce a macroexternality of consumption. That is, the welfare of an agent is affected by an additive externality to which all agents (or a nonnegligible group of consumers) contribute. To be more specific, we add another argument to the utility function, namely the aggregate consumption of y, $\int_A y d\mu$.

The optimization problem of a selfish consumer is then

$$\text{Max}_{(x,y)} \; U\left(x, y, \int_A yd\mu\right)$$

subject to

$$x + (1/\alpha)y = 1 + (1/\alpha)1,$$

which gives the first-order condition $U_2/U_1 = 1/\alpha$.

The consumer in this example has a noncooperative, or parametric, behavior with respect to the amount of the externality. It is well known that the outcome of such a noncooperative economy is inefficient. The marginal conditions of the Pareto optimum with equal distribution are $U_2/U_1 = 1/\alpha - U_3/U_1$. Now assume that we have changed the ethics of the typical agent so that when he maximizes his utility function he assumes that everybody behaves as he does. When he chooses the quantity y of good 2, he then assumes that $\int_A yd\mu = y$, so his maximization problem becomes

$$\text{Max}_y \; U(1 + 1/\alpha - (1/\alpha)y, y, y)$$

for which the marginal conditions are $U_2/U_1 = 1/\alpha - U_3/U_1$.

This Kantian behavior realizes the optimum that would be attained with selfish behavior only if appropriate taxes $t = -U_3/U_1$ were imposed on the consumption of good y.

This formalization seems satisfactory for the example of the beach, in which case the solution of taxation is clearly irrelevant. The choice is then between two solutions. One is to adopt a repressive policy that necessitates an expensive control system (or requires extremely high penalties) and is not flexible enough to allow fine tuning toward an optimum. Such a policy allows only rules that are prohibitions. Another possibility is to accept the (radical?) idea that preferences and behaviors are endogenous to the system and to try by means of an information campaign to induce a Kantian type of behavior, even if a negligible number of consumers do not comply. When the economic development of the Middle Ages required honest practices among merchants, a new ethics helped by some coercive legislation appeared. Even if it may seem dangerous to some humanists, we can predict that future societies will sometimes use the formidable power of modern news media and governmental authority to impose this type of solution.

I want to emphasize the connection between the relevance of a new ethics and the existence of macroeconomic constraints different from the usual additive constraints. The following sections consider more sophisticated models and show how different problems can be articulated in relation to questions such as, Does a new macroeconomic constraint exist? Do people take it into account?

DEPENDENT RANDOMNESS AND MACROECONOMIC CONSTRAINTS

Consider an infinite succession of overlapping generations of identical consumers who live for two periods. The total population of "young" and "old" consumers is constant. In the first period of his life a consumer faces no uncertainty but in the second period he faces S different states of nature. A state of nature defines an endowment of good 0 (which is for simplicity the only good in the endowment). Let $w_s > 0$ be the endowment of good 0 in period 1 if $s = 0$ and in state s of period 2 if $s = 1, 2, \ldots, S$.

In period 1 a consumer can buy goods to consume in this period. This consumption may modify his probabilities of being in a certain state in the second period. Let $x_s \in R^L$ (L is the number of goods) be the consumption vector for a consumer in period 1 if $s = 0$, in state s of period 2 if $s = 1, \ldots, S$.

The probability of being in state s, for $s = 1, \ldots, S$, is π_s, which is now a function of x_0.

There is no forward market for goods, but in period 1 a consumer can buy insurance against state $s = 1, \ldots, S$, at price q_s. Let z_s be the amount of claims against state s bought (if positive) or sold short (if negative) by a representative consumer. The technology is a simple fixed-coefficients technology with no lag in production so that the price of good l is p_l, $l = 1, \ldots, L$. The price of good 0 is normalized to 1.

Considering only stationary states and assuming expected

utility behavior, we see that the maximization problem of a consumer is then

$$\text{Max} \sum_{s=1}^{S} \pi_s(x_0)V(x_0, x_s)$$

subject to

$$px_0 \leqq w_0 - \sum_{s=1}^{S} q_s z_s,$$

$$px_s \leqq w_s + z_s, \qquad s = 1, \ldots, S,$$
$$x_s \geqq 0, \qquad\qquad s = 0, 1, \ldots, S.$$

For simplicity assume that there is one insurance company with a zero-profit constraint. This requirement is made possible by having the number of consumers go to infinity so that frequencies in all states of nature converge to probabilities.

It is then possible to show the existence of a stationary equilibrium that is in general inefficient. We simplify a little by ignoring the usual nonconcavity of the expected utility function and assuming that all consumers choose the same action in the first period of their life. Then at the equilibrium the price of insurance will be such that $q_s = \pi_s(x_0)$. The choice of x_0 by a consumer has two effects, one on his own probability distribution and utility function, and another, which is negligible from his point of view, on the price of insurance. The macroeconomic constraints of the problem are the terms of the insurance contracts, which can be changed by collective behavior, and the origin of the inefficiency is that individual behavior does not take these constraints into account.

The efficient solution suggested in chapter 3, namely a variable insurance premium $q_s = \pi_s(x_0)$ is strictly equivalent in this model to a form of Kantian behavior.

NEUTRALITY OF MONEY AND MACROECONOMIC CONSTRAINT

This last example is from David Starrett (1973a), who shows the relevance of the macroeconomic constraint discussion in a traditional problem. Consider an economy where overlapping generations live for two periods and the population is stationary, as in the preceding section. In the first period of his life a consumer receives wages w and transfers t from the government in the form of money. He can consume (there is only one good) c_1, hold money m with a real return r_m, or hold an asset a (capital in a firm) with a stochastic return r. In the second period he consumes (c_2) his receipts from money holdings $r_m m$ and from his asset holdings ra.

The maximization program of a consumer is then

$$\text{Max } U(c_1) + EU(c_2)$$

subject to

$$c_1 = w + t - a - m,$$
$$c_2 = r_m m + ra.$$

Let M be the nominal per capita quantity of money, m the real per capita quantity of money, and P the price level. Starrett focuses on stationary states for which $\Delta m/m = 0$. By definition $r_m - 1 = -\Delta p/p = \Delta m/m - \Delta M/M$, and $\Delta m/m = 0$ implies $\Delta M/P = m(1 - r_m)$.

Starrett made assumptions on the technology such that the return on the asset is stochastic at the individual level but not at the macro level. For example, there is technological uncertainty at the level of the firm, but the law of large numbers eliminates the uncertainty at the macro level.

A macroeconomic constraint relates the per capita transfer to young consumers t to the amount of real money created by the government:

$$t = \Delta M/P = m(1 - r_m).$$

Starrett then shows that a stationary state corresponds to each policy of the government. Neutrality of money is defined as the government's inability to affect the long-run equilibrium. The crucial question about the neutrality of money is then, Are consumers aware of the relation between the transfers they receive and the rate of inflation? If they are aware of this relation, their maximization program becomes

$$\text{Max } U(c_1) + EU(r_m m + ra)$$

subject to

$$c_1 + a + m = w + t = w + m(1 - r_m)$$

or

$$c_1 + a + r_m m = w.$$

Then the real yield of money turns out to be 1, whatever the government does. Money is neutral. I do not suggest that consumers behave this way (Starrett 1973); this is a question of fact, but I emphasize (and it was noted by Starrett) the relevance of the question whether people take into account the macroeconomic constraint.

CONCLUSION

We could consider many more examples. The average quality of a good such as in chapter 1 can be considered a macroeconomic constraint. The problem of optimal tax evasion might be examined together with the idea of a budgetary constraint for the government, so that if consumers suffer disutility by paying taxes, the presence of cheating which induces higher taxes creates an inefficiency at the macro level. To illustrate the argument I ignored all distribution problems by assuming that people are alike. Assuming heterogeneity creates difficulties for the definition of modes of Kantian behavior, at least at the operational level. We can expect to realize the positive aspects of Kantian behavior in cases in which social interest conflicts to some reasonable degree with private interest. In particular it seems possible to ask people, with some hope of success, to make nonfinancial sacrifices (such as putting garbage into cans, saving energy, and the like). However, I would not wager on the success of a campaign to convince people not to cheat on their tax returns. But then it may be that I am still a pessimistic neoclassical economist.

PART II
A General Theory of Self-Protection

The theory of demand for insurance has been the topic of a large number of papers (Gould 1969; Mossin 1968; Pashigian, Schkade, and Menefee 1966; Smith 1968) that have adopted the Bernouilli-Ramsey framework of decision making under uncertainty. Unfortunately, until very recently this neat framework led investigators to overlook two basic features of uncertainty relevant to the study of insurance, namely the dependence of utility functions on nonmonetary factors and the possibility that agents can influence probabilities of identifiable states of nature. The first point has been made vigorously by Hirshleifer (1970), and a clear reconciliation with the Von Neumann–Morgenstern approach can be found in Arrow (1974), in which he extends the classical demand analysis for insurance to state-dependent utility functions. The second point has been introduced in the economics literature by Arrow (1963) using the somewhat misleading term moral hazard, which is now common in the insurance profession (see also the comment by Pauly, 1968, and Arrow's reply, 1968). A thorough demand analysis for this case has been given by Ehrlich and Becker (1972), who refer to it as self-protection. They call self-insurance the actions taken by agents that modify incomes in the different states of nature.

In a general equilibrium context Malinvaud (1972, 1973) has

called attention to the special features of individual risks, which are precisely the risks dealt with by insurance. He also mentioned the necessity of using state-dependent utility functions. Of interest here is his (sketchy) result that in the case of individual risks, markets for sure goods supplemented by an insurance system realize a Pareto optimum, avoiding the large number of markets necessary in an Arrow-Debreu economy (Arrow 1963–64, Debreu 1959, Radner 1968).

The purpose of part II is to study the general equilibrium consequences of moral hazard.

In chapter 3, using a simple model of overlapping generations, I show why moral hazard may upset the existence of an equilibrium and I give conditions that ensure its existence. This equilibrium is, in general, globally and even locally inefficient. The proposed solutions to these inefficiencies require a large amount of information.

In chapter 4 I show that this existence problem can be solved in a slightly different framework. To overcome the excessive information requirements of the first-best solutions given in chapter 3, I introduce a court as an economic agent and study the possibility of implementing Pareto optima with the use of penalties.

3

Moral Hazard in a General Equilibrium Framework

In the model of overlapping generations developed in this chapter, a young consumer may affect, by his economic behavior, the probability distribution over the states of nature that he faces in the second period of his life.

Focusing on the study of stationary states justifies the use of objective probabilities but also presents two types of difficulties. First, stationary equilibria may not exist, even with an infinite number of agents, unless we make very strong assumptions. Second, when they exist, these stationary equilibria are generally inefficient. Economic policies may be devised to deal with this inefficiency.

Description of the Economy

Consumers who are all identical (the generalization to several types is straightforward) live for two periods, and in each generation there are N consumers. Assume that the growth rate of the population is zero, but the same analysis could be carried out with a positive rate of growth. The population at any date is $2N$.

In the first period of their lives consumers bear no risk. However, they can find themselves in one of S different states of nature in the second period. Each consumer is assigned an index h ($h = 1$ if he is young, $h = 2$ if he is old), an index s (indicating which state he is in if he is old; $s = 1, \ldots, S$), and an index i (to define his identity, $i = 1, \ldots, N$). We will often use a representative consumer and omit the index i.

Assume that there is only one good at each date.[1] Let w_1 be the endowment in period 1, and let w_2^s, $s = 1, \ldots, S$, be the endowment in state s of period 2.

Assumption 1. $w_1 \geq 0, w_2^s \geq 0, s = 1, \ldots, S$, with at least one strict inequality.

In the first period of his life every consumer faces a probability distribution over the states of nature in his second period of life. Let π_s be the probability that a consumer will be in state s in the second period of his life. Obviously, $\pi^s \geq 0, s = 1, \ldots, S$, and $\sum_{s=1}^{S} \pi^s = 1$. Apart from eventually providing satisfaction, consumption in the first period may influence the probabilities π^s, $s = 1, \ldots, S$. Consequently $\pi = (\pi^1, \pi^2, \ldots, \pi^S)$ is a function defined on R with values in the simplex of R^S. Preferences of a representative consumer are defined on the space $X = R_+ \times R_+^S$ of feasible consumption paths. Assume that they satisfy a generalized expected utility hypothesis such that his objective function is (see appendix 3.A for a detailed discussion of this assumption)

$$V(x_1, x_2^1, \ldots, x_2^S) = \sum_{s=1}^{S} \pi^s(x_1)U^s(x_1, x_2^s),$$

where x_1 is consumption in period 1 and x_2^s, $s = 1, \ldots, S$, is consumption in state s of period 2. Let $x = (x_1, x_2^1, \ldots, x_2^S)$.

Assumption 2.   For $s = 1, \ldots, S$, the functions π^s and U^s are continuous.

---

1. We could have several goods, but this would complicate the analysis without increasing our understanding of the problems that we want to focus on in this chapter.

Assumption 3. $\text{Min}_{x_1 \geq 0} \, \pi^s(x_1) \geq \underline{\pi} > 0$ for $s = 1, \ldots, S$.[2]

Assumption 4. There exists $s^* \in \{1, \ldots, S\}$ such that $U^s(x_1, x_2^s)$ is increasing in x_2^s.

Let I be the segment $[\underline{\pi}, 1]$, and let I^S be the Cartesian product of S times I.

There exist only spot markets of the good. However, in the first period of his life a consumer can buy claims on the good in a specific state of nature in the second period of his life (insurance). Such a possibility exists for each state of nature. At the same price he can also borrow in the first period, with the obligation of repayment, only if a specific state occurs.[3] These transactions are made with insurance companies. Let z^s be the amount of claims against state s bought by a representative consumer (z^s can be positive or negative), and let q^s be the price of a claim against state s. Let $z = (z^1, \ldots, z^S)$ and $q = (q^1, \ldots, q^S)$.

Behavior of Agents

CONSUMERS

We can express the optimization program of a young consumer at date t as

$$\text{Max } V(x_1, x_2^1, \ldots, x_2^S) = \sum_{s=1}^{S} \pi^s(x_1) U^s(x_1, x_2^s) \qquad (3.1)$$

2. This assumption implies that no action of the agent can prevent the occurrence of a state of nature (even in the limit). It is a simple way to avoid unboundedness problems of a St. Petersburg paradox nature. Otherwise, the consumer might have utility in consuming infinite amounts in states with probability zero. As usual, another solution to this problem would be to bound the utility functions.

3. The assumption of one price for positive and negative insurance can be criticized. In a temporary equilibrium analysis where bankruptcies are possible, risk of default should be taken into account and there is an obvious asymmetry between an individual and an insurance company which pools risks. However, since we are interested only in competitive stationary equilibria, the assumption is appropriate.

subject to

$$x_1 + \sum_{s=1}^{S} q^s z^s \leq w_1,$$

$$x_2^s \leq w_2^s + z^s, \qquad s = 1, \ldots, S,$$
$$x_1 \geq 0, \quad x_2^s \geq 0, \qquad s = 1, \ldots, S.$$

The constraints of problem 3.1 can be rewritten as

$$x_1 + \sum_{s=1}^{S} q^s x_2^s \leq w_1 + \sum_{s=1}^{S} q^s w_2^s, \qquad (3.2)$$

$$x_1 \geq 0, \quad x_2^s \geq 0, \qquad s = 1, \ldots, S.$$

Let $B(q) = \{x | x_1 + \Sigma_{s=1}^{S} q^s x_2^s \leq w_1 + \Sigma_{s=1}^{S} q^s w_2^s, x \geq 0\}$. The optimization problem 3.1 is then simply

$$\text{Max } V(x), \qquad x \in B(q). \qquad (3.3)$$

The trivial optimization program of an old consumer in state $s, s = 1, \ldots, S$, at date t, is

$$\text{Max } U^s(x_1^*, x_2^s) \qquad (3.4)$$

subject to

$$x_2^s \leq w_2^s + z^{*s}, \qquad x_2^s \geq 0,$$

where (x_1^*, z^{*s}) have been chosen in the previous period.

INSURANCE COMPANIES

Insurance companies agree to sell or buy the claims of consumers at prices $q^s, s = 1, \ldots, S$. The firm receives (or lends if negative) $q^s z^s$ from a young consumer and pays him (or receives from him) z^s in the second period if an event of probability π^s occurs.

For each type of contract (which means one type of risk s, $s = 1, \ldots, S$) the cash flow of an insurance company in period t is

$$P_t q^s(t) z^s(t) - f_t^s P_{t-1} z^s(t-1)$$

where P_t is the number of young consumers who contract

and P_{t-1} the number of (now old) consumers who contracted last period. The term f_t^s is the proportion of old consumers who face state s in period t. In this formulation of profit the assumption is that all the individuals who contract with this company have exactly the same behavior. However, this assumption need not hold. We shall therefore be led to an examination of different institutional assumptions about the insurance companies.

Assumption 5. There is perfect competition among insurance companies.

The intent of assumption 5 is to imply more than is usually meant by perfect competition. Specifically, if the number N of young consumers goes to infinity, then the number of consumers insured by any company on each type of contract must also go to infinity (or is zero for all companies). This assumption can be heuristically justified for the analysis of stationary equilibria as follows. If an insurance company has a finite number of consumers and imposes the same type of contract as other companies with an infinite number, in the long run it will have negative profits in some periods and will fail. If its contracts are not as good, then it will lack consumers and fail as a result of competition.

Thus if all young consumers consume the same amount of goods in period 1 of their lives, frequencies f_t^s, $s = 1, \ldots ,$ S, converge to probabilities π^s for each company (Malinvaud 1972).

Alternatively, we can choose the following assumptions.

Assumption 5′. There exists a unique insurance company with an institutional zero-profit constraint on each type of contract.

Assumption 5″. There exists a unique insurance company with an institutional overall zero-profit constraint.

The existence of insurance companies allows consumers to transfer purchasing power from period 1 to period 2 of their lives, conditional on the occurence of some states of nature, and vice versa. Forward markets conditional on states of nature would provide the same opportunities, but the structure of generations is such that these markets cannot emerge. An institutional solution to this deficiency is needed.

Existence of Stationary Equilibria

To study the existence of stationary equilibria we let N go to infinity so that frequencies converge to probabilities and uncertainty disappears at the macro level.[4]

The price of the good is normalized to 1. Let Q be the price space of insurance contracts, $Q = \{q | q^s \geqq 0, s = 1, \ldots, S\}$.

There are two crucial features of this model. First, the expected utility functions are generally not quasi-concave. Second, the feasible set is endogenous to the model, since it depends on consumption by young consumers; moreover it is generally not convex. These features lead to important difficulties in the existence proofs. To have maximum flexibility we allow different behavior for identical consumers. The proportion of consumers with consumption vector x^δ is denoted by λ^δ.

Definition. A *strong stationary equilibrium* is a finite set Δ, a set of positive weights λ^δ, $\delta \in \Delta$, adding up to 1, a price vector $\bar{q} \in Q$, a set of consumption vectors $\bar{x}^\delta = (\bar{x}_1^\delta, \bar{x}_2^{1\delta}, \ldots, \bar{x}_2^{S\delta})$, $\delta \in \Delta$, such that

$$\sum_{\delta \in \Delta} \lambda^\delta \bar{q}^s (\bar{x}_2^{s\delta} - w_2^s) - \sum_{\delta \in \Delta} \lambda^\delta \pi^s(\bar{x}_1^\delta)(\bar{x}_2^{s\delta} - w_2^s) = 0$$

$$\text{for } s = 1, \ldots, S, \quad (3.5)$$

$$\sum_{\delta \in \Delta} \lambda^\delta (\bar{x}_1^\delta - w_1) + \sum_{\delta \in \Delta} \lambda^\delta \sum_{s=1}^{S} \pi^s(\bar{x}_1^\delta)(\bar{x}_2^{s\delta} - w_2^s) = 0, \quad (3.6)$$

$$\bar{x}^\delta = (\bar{x}_1^\delta, \bar{x}_2^{1\delta}, \ldots, \bar{x}_2^{S\delta}) \in \xi(\bar{q}) = \{x^* | V(x^*)$$
$$= \text{Max } V(x) \text{ for } x \in B(\bar{q})\} \quad \text{for all } \delta \in \Delta. \quad (3.7)$$

In a strong equilibrium there is zero profit, with probabil-

---

4. The most appropriate framework would be an economy with a continuum of consumers. See chapter 4.

ity one, on each type of contract (condition 3.5). Condition (3.6) assures equilibrium on the good market. Condition (3.7) is self-explanatory.

In a *weak equilibrium* condition 3.5 is replaced by

$$\sum_{s=1}^{S} \sum_{\delta \in \Delta} \lambda^\delta \bar{q}^s (\bar{x}_2^{s\delta} - w_2^s) - \sum_{s=1}^{S} \sum_{\delta \in \Delta} \lambda^\delta \pi^s (x_1^\delta)(x_2^{s\delta} - w_2^s) = 0, \quad (3.8)$$

that is, there is only an overall zero-profit constraint.

If Δ is reduced to a single element, then all consumers have the same behavior. We will refer to such equilibria as *uniform* (strong or weak) equilibria.

The uniform strong equilibrium is particularly interesting because it allows genuine competition among insurance companies. If an equilibrium is strong but not uniform, it may be destroyed by the Rothschild-Stiglitz argument (1972), if companies are allowed to compete on price-quantity contracts. In this case companies attempt to attract the consumers with the lowest risks and contract with them by proposing contracts that only the low-risk consumer would desire. The Rothschild-Stiglitz argument is even more convincing for the weak equilibrium; in that case insurance companies can easily choose the best type of contract to destroy equilibrium.

The concept of strong equilibrium appears then to be compatible with competition (with the preceding qualification), but the concept of weak equilibrium is only compatible with the existence of one insurance company.

To prove existence of a stationary equilibrium we need a strong assumption.

Assumption 6. The utility function $V(x)$ is quasi-concave.[5]

5. This assumption would be satisfied if the probability functions, $\pi^s(\cdot)$, $s = 1, \ldots, S$, were constant valued and the (Von Neumann) utility functions $U^s(\cdot, \cdot)$, $s = 1, \ldots, S$, were concave. However, the dependence of probabilities on x_1 may disturb the quasi concavity. In particular, it requires that the dependence of probabilities on x_1 not destroy the existence of decreasing marginal rates of substitution between x_1 and x_2^s, $s = 1, \ldots, S$.

Proposition 3.1. Under assumptions 1–6 there exists a uniform strong equilibrium.

Proof. Restrict the price vector q to the compact set $I^S = [\underline{\pi}, 1]^S$. Since $V(x)$ is quasi-concave, then under assumptions 1–4 the demand correspondence of a representative consumer is an upper hemicontinuous (uhc), nonempty, convex, compact-valued correspondence $\xi(q)$ from I^S into R_+^{S+1} (Debreu 1959). Its domain is included in a compact convex set C.

The probability $\pi(x)$ is a continuous function from C into I^S. Let ψ be the uhc correspondence with nonempty, convex, compact values from the convex compact set $C \times I^S$ into itself, defined as $\psi(x, q) = [\xi(q), \pi(x)]$. By Kakutani's theorem it has a fixed point $q^* = \pi(x^*)$ for $x^* \in \xi(q^*)$. Hence conditions (3.6) and (3.7) are satisfied. With assumption 4 Walras's law is satisfied for (x^*, q^*), so condition (3.2) is also fulfilled. QED

It is clear that a (uniform) strong equilibrium is also a (uniform) weak equilibrium.

The assumption of quasi concavity of the expected utility function is certainly very strong. However, it is necessary in order to prove existence of an equilibrium, even though we have a large number of consumers, a rather surprising result.

Proposition 3.2. Under assumptions 1–5 there need not exist an equilibrium, either strong or weak.

Proof. We construct an example in which $V(x)$ is not quasi-concave and there is no equilibrium. Let

$$S = 2, \quad w_1 > 10, \quad w_2^1 > 0, \quad w_2^2 > 0,$$
$$U^1(x_1, x_2^1) = x_1 + \tfrac{1}{2}x_2^1,$$
$$U^2(x_1, x_2^2) = x_1,$$
$$\pi^1(x_1) = 0.9 - 0.1x_1, \quad \text{if } 0 \leqq x_1 \leqq 8,$$
$$= 0.1, \qquad\qquad \text{if } x_1 \geqq 8.$$

The consumer seeks to

$$\text{Max } x_1 + \tfrac{1}{2}\pi^1(x_1)x_2^1$$

subject to

$$x_1 + q^1 x_2^1 + q^2 x_2^2 \leqq w_1 + q^1 w_2^1 + q^2 w_2^2,$$
$$x_1, x_2^1, x_2^2 \geqq 0.$$

Obviously $x_2^{2*} = 0$.

Figure 3.1 shows a map of indifference curves. For $q^1 < \frac{9}{20}$

$$x_1^* = 0, \qquad x_2^{1*} = (w_1 + q^2 w_2^1 + q^2 w_2^2)/q^1.$$

For $q^1 > \frac{9}{20}$

$$x_1^* = w_1 + q^1 w_2^1 + q^2 w_2^2, \qquad x_2^{1*} = 0.$$

We first observe that in these two cases a strong equilibrium is impossible. If $q^1 < \frac{9}{20}$, then $x_1^* = 0$ implies $\pi^1(x_1^*) = 0.9$, which is larger than q^1. Moreover, the contract is active, since

Fig. 3.1

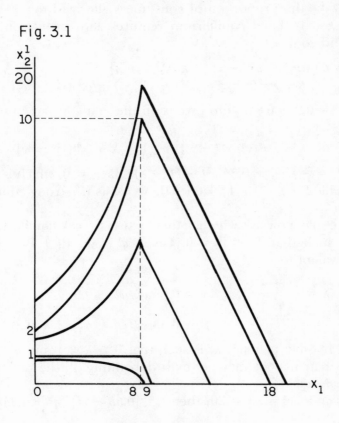

$z^1 = x_2^1 - w_2^1 = (w_1 + q^2 w_2^2)/q^1 > 0$. On this contract the insurance company would lose money.

If $q^1 > \frac{9}{20}$, then $x_1^* = w_1 + q^1 w_2^1 + q^2 w_2^2$ is larger than 8 if, for example, $w_1 = 10$. Therefore $\pi^1(x_1^*) = 0.1$; since this contract is active, $z^{1^*} = x_2^{1^*} - w_2^1 = -w_2^1 < 0$, the insurance company would also lose money because consumers would buy negative insurance.

The remaining possibility is the existence of a nonuniform strong equilibrium for $q_?^1 = \frac{9}{20}$. We distribute consumers among the two consumption vectors

$$(x_1^a, x_2^{1a}) = \left(0, \frac{w_1 + q^1 w_2^1 + q^2 w_2^2}{q^1}\right),$$

$$(x_1^b, x_2^{1b}) = (w_1 + q^1 w_2^1 + q^2 w_2^2, 0).$$

Let λ be the proportion of consumers allocated to (x_1^a, x_2^{1a}), $0 < \lambda < 1$. Then equilibrium requires zero profits on the second contract

$$\mathbf{P}_2 = q^2[\lambda(x_2^{2a} - w_2^2) + (1 - \lambda)(x_2^{2b} - w_2^2)]$$
$$- \lambda\pi^2(x_1^a)(x_2^{2a} - w_2^2) - (1 - \lambda)\pi^2(x_1^b)(x_2^{2b} - w_2^2) = 0,$$

or $q^2 = 0.9 - 0.8\lambda$. Zero profits on the first contract imply

$$\mathbf{P}_1 = q^1[\lambda(x_2^{1a} - w_2^1) + (1 - \lambda)(x_2^{1b} - w_2^1)]$$
$$- \lambda\pi^1(x_1^a)(x_2^{1a} - w_2^1) - (1 - \lambda)\pi^1(x_1^b)(x_2^{1b} - w_2^1) = 0,$$

or $\mathbf{P}_1 = -\lambda[w_1 + 0.55w_2^2] - (1 - \lambda)0.35w_2^1 = 0$, which is impossible for $\lambda \in [0, 1]$. Hence there exists no strong equilibrium.

We may now ask whether there exists a weak equilibrium, one such that $\mathbf{P}_1 + \mathbf{P}_2 = 0$. Given $q^1 = \frac{9}{20}$, $\mathbf{P}_1 + \mathbf{P}_2 = 0$ is equivalent to

$$\lambda = -\frac{q^2 + \alpha}{q^2 + \beta}, \qquad \alpha = 0.35w_2^1/w_2^2 - 0.9,$$

$$\beta = 0.35w_2^1/w_2^2 - w_1/w_2^2 + 0.8.$$

A feasible pair (q^2, λ) is such that $0 \leqq \lambda \leqq 1$ and $q^2 \geqq 0$. This pair may or may not exist depending on the values of w_1, w_1^2, w_2^2.

If $w_1 = w_2^1 = w_2^2 = 20$, then $(q^2, [0.55 - q^2]/[q^2 + 1.45])$ is feasible if $0.1 \leqq q^2 \leqq 0.55$. For example, $q^1 = 0.45$, $q^2 = 0.35$, $\lambda = \frac{1}{9}$ is a weak nonuniform equilibrium. However, if $w_1 = 20$, $w_2^1 = 40$, $w_2^2 = 10$, then there is no weak equilibrium because $\lambda = (-q^2 + 0.5)/0.2 < 0$ for all $q^2 \geqq 0$. It is easy to check that there exists no such equilibrium for $q^2 > \frac{9}{20}$ and $q^2 < \frac{9}{20}$.   QED

It is remarkable that even a weak nonuniform equilibrium may not exist even though the number of consumers is infinite. The economic reason for the nonexistence of an equilibrium in the numerical example is the following one. When the price of insurance for state 1 is below 0.45, consumers buy positive insurance but do not self-protect themselves. Thus the probability of state 1 is high, and the insurance company suffers losses. When the price of insurance for state 1 is above 0.45, the nonconvexity of preferences leads to a complete change of behavior. Consumers buy *negative* insurance and self-protect themselves at the maximum rate, again resulting in losses for the insurance company. When the insurance premium is exactly 0.45, consumers are indifferent between these two types of behavior, and since the insurance company suffers losses under each type of behavior, it suffers losses independently of the distribution of consumers between the two types of behavior. Technically, the value of the aggregate excess net demand is not necessarily negative; this latter property is obtained by summing individual budget constraints in the classical theory of value, but does not hold with individual risks.

Inefficiency of Stationary Equilibria

Among the class of stationary states, competitive equilibria need not be efficient. Different heuristic interpretations of this result are possible.

Definition.   A stationary allocation $[\Delta, (\lambda^\delta), (x^\delta)]$ is feasible if

1. Δ is a finite set and $\lambda^\delta > 0$ for all $\delta \in \Delta$ with $\Sigma_{\delta \in \Delta} \lambda^\delta = 1$.
2. $x^\delta \geq 0$ for all $\delta \in \Delta$ and $\Sigma_{\delta \in \Delta} \lambda^\delta [(x_1^\delta - w_1) + \Sigma_{s=1}^S \pi^s(x_1^\delta)(x_2^{s\delta} - w_2^s)] \leqq 0$.

Definition.   A stationary allocation $[\Delta^*, (\lambda^{\delta^*}), (x^{\delta^*})]$ is efficient if

1. It is feasible.
2. There exists no other feasible allocation $[\Delta, (\lambda^{\delta}), (x^{\delta})]$ such that Δ can be partitioned into Δ^* subsets Δ^{δ^*}, $\delta^* \in \Delta^*$, such that

a. $\Sigma_{\delta \in \Delta^{\delta^*}} \lambda^{\delta} = \lambda^{\delta^*}$ for all $\delta^* \in \Delta^*$.

b. $V(x^{\delta}) \geqq V(x^{\delta^*})$ for all $\delta^* \in \Delta^*$, $\delta \in \Delta^{\delta^*}$, with strict inequality for at least one pair $(\delta^{*\prime}, \delta^{\prime}) \in \Delta^* \times \Delta^{\delta^{*\prime}}$.

Proposition 3.3.   Under assumptions 1–6 a stationary equilibrium need not be efficient.

Proof.   We construct an example of an inefficient stationary equilibrium. Let

$$S = 2, \qquad U^1(x_1, x_2^1) = x_2^1, \qquad U^2(x_1, x_2^2) = 0,$$
$$\pi^1(x_1) = 0.1(1 + x_1) \quad \text{for } 0 \leqq x_1 \leqq 8,$$
$$\qquad\qquad = 0.9 \qquad\qquad \text{for} \qquad x_1 \geqq 8,$$
$$w_1 = w_2^1 = 5, \qquad w_2^2 = 3.$$

By proposition 3.1 there exists a uniform strong equilibrium. The price vector $(q^1, q^2) = (0.5, 0.5)$ and the allocation $(x_1, x_2^1, x_2^2) = (4, 10, 0)$ form a uniform strong equilibrium. The level of utility obtained is $U(4, 10, 0) = 5$.

However, the feasible set of uniform per capita consumption vectors is

$$F = \{(x_1, x_2^1, x_2^2) \geqq 0 | (x_1 - 5) + \pi^1(x_1)(x_2^1 - 5)$$
$$+ \pi^2(x_1)(x_2^2 - 3) \leqq 0\}.$$

The stationary allocation $(0, 82, 0)$ is therefore feasible and gives a higher level of utility $U(0, 82, 0) = 8.2$.

The crucial point is that the feasible set is endogenous and that decentralized behavior may lead to a "bad" feasible set (figure 3.2).   QED

This example might suggest that the stationary equilibrium is globally inefficient but locally efficient.[6] Assuming

6. The inefficiency is not due to the nonconvexity of the feasible set that exists in this example. Another example with convex preferences and a

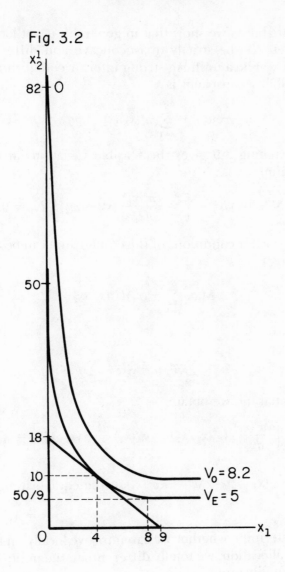

Fig. 3.2

convex feasible set is obtained with

$$S = 2, \quad w_1 = w_2^1 = w_2^2 = 10,$$
$$\pi^1(x_1) = 0.9 - 0.8 \exp\{-x_1\},$$
$$U^1(x_1, x_2^1) = x_2^1, \quad U^2(x_1, x_2^2) = x_2^2.$$

differentiability, we show that in general it is not locally efficient. Let $V(x)$ be strictly quasi-concave and differentiable, and let $(\bar{q}, \bar{x})$ be a uniform strong interior equilibrium. Then the feasibility constraint is

$$(x_1 - w_1) + \sum_{s=1}^{S} \pi^s(x_1)(x_2^s - w_2^s) = 0. \qquad (3.9)$$

Differentiating 3.9 gives the feasible variations around the equilibrium

$$dx_1 + \sum_{s=1}^{S} \pi^s(x_1)dx_2^s + \left[\sum_{s=1}^{S} \frac{d\pi^s(x_1)}{dx_1} (x_2^s - w_2^s)\right] dx_1 = 0. \qquad (3.10)$$

The first-order conditions of the equilibrium can be obtained by solving

$$\text{Max} \sum_{s=1}^{S} \pi^s(x_1)U^s(x_1, x_2^s)$$

subject to

$$x_1 + \sum_{s=1}^{S} q^s x_2^s \leqq w_1 + \sum_{s=1}^{S} q^s w_2^s.$$

Differentiating, we obtain

$$\sum_{s=1}^{S} \left[\frac{d\pi^s(x_1)}{dx_1} U^s(x_1, x_2^s) + \pi^s(x_1) \frac{\partial U^s}{\partial x_1} (x_1, x_2^s)\right] = \lambda, \qquad (3.11)$$

$$\pi^s(x_1) \frac{\partial U^s}{\partial x_2^s} (x_1, x_2^s) = \lambda q^s = \lambda \pi^s(x_1) \text{ at the equilibrium,}$$

$$s = 1, \ldots, S.$$

To determine whether we can improve locally on the equilibrium allocation, we totally differentiate the utility function at the equilibrium

$$\sum_{s=1}^{S} \left[\frac{d\pi^s(x_1)}{dx_1} \cdot U^s(x_1, x_s^2) + \pi^s(x_1) \frac{\partial U^s}{\partial x_1} (x_1, x_2^s)\right] dx_1$$

$$+ \sum_{s=1}^{S} \pi^s(x_1) \frac{\partial U^s}{\partial x_2^s} (x_1, x_2^s)dx_2^s. \qquad (3.12)$$

Substituting 3.11 into 3.12 gives

$$\lambda dx_1 + \lambda \sum_{s=1}^{S} \pi^s(x_1)dx_2^s, \tag{3.13}$$

and substituting 3.10 into 3.13 gives

$$-\lambda \left[\sum_{s=1}^{S} \frac{d\pi^s(x_1)}{dx_1} (x_2^s - w_2^s) \right] dx_1. \tag{3.14}$$

We know that λ, the marginal utility of income, is positive. For $dx_1 > 0$, $\sum_{s=1}^{S}[d\pi^s(x_1)/dx_1](x_2^s - w_s^2)$ may clearly be negative with a suitable probability function. Therefore the equilibrium may be locally inefficient. Note two special cases. If π^s is constant, $s = 1, \ldots, S$, then expression 3.14 vanishes. If $x_2^s - w_2^s = a$ for all s, then

$$\sum_{s=1}^{S} \frac{d\pi^s(x_1)}{dx_1} (x_2^s - w_2^s) = a \sum_{s=1}^{S} \frac{d\pi^s(x_1)}{dx_1} = 0$$

since $\sum_{s=1}^{S} \pi^s(x_1) = 1$ for all x_1.

In a further attempt to clarify the issue, we provide an analogy with classical externalities. We may regard the insurance company as a producer whose input is one unit of the good in period 1 and whose output is a joint product of α^1 units of the good in state 1, α^2 units in state 2, $\ldots$, α^S units in state S of period 2. The surrogate production function is given by the budget constraint of the insurance company, so we have

$$\alpha^s = \frac{1}{\pi^s(x_1)}, \qquad \sum_{s=1}^{S} \frac{1}{\alpha^s} = 1$$

where x_1 is the per capita consumption of young individuals.

Clearly the individual's behavior now influences the technical coefficients of the producer insurance company. Therefore our problem can be viewed as a consumption externality on production. When there are large numbers of individuals, it is rational for one individual to disregard his impact (which is negligible) on these technical coefficients.

Self-Insurance versus Self-Protection

The impact of consumption on the probabilities has been referred to in the literature (Ehrlich and Becker 1972) as *self-protection*. The direct impact of consumption in the first period on endowments in the second period has similarly been defined as *self-insurance*. The analysis of self-insurance is much simpler than the study of self-protection, at least in the one commodity model considered here.

With the same notations as before, the optimization program of a consumer can now be written as

$$\text{Max} \sum_{s=1}^{S} \pi^s U^s(x_1, x_2^s)$$

subject to

$$x_1 + \sum_{s=1}^{S} q^s z^s \leqq w_1,$$

$$x_2 \leqq w_2^s(x_1) + z^s, \qquad s = 1, \ldots, S,$$
$$x_1 \geqq 0, \quad x_2^s \geqq 0, \qquad s = 1, \ldots, S. \qquad (3.15)$$

These constraints may be rewritten as

$$x_1 + \sum_{s=1}^{S} q^s x_2^s \leqq w_1 + \sum_{s=1}^{S} q^s w_2^s(x_1). \qquad (3.16)$$

Assumption 7. $w_1 > 0$, $w_2^s(x_1) \geqq 0$, $s = 1, \ldots, S$, for all $x_1 \geqq 0$.

Moreover w_2^s is a continuous function of x_1, which is bounded above for $s = 1, \ldots, S$. The probability distribution of states of the world faced by a young consumer is now fixed.

Since insurance companies cannot discriminate among consumers and since all consumers present the same risk, the only possible strong equilibrium price vector is $q^s = \pi^s$, $s = 1, \ldots, S$.

Proposition 3.4. Under assumptions 2–5 and 7 there exists a stationary strong equilibrium.

Proof. For $q^s = \pi^s$, $s = 1, \ldots, S$, the budget set is a fixed (eventually nonconvex) compact set. The maximization of the continuous function $V(x)$ on this set leads to a set of maxima. Any such point or any convex combination of such points is an equilibrium (the feasibility constraint is satisfied by Walras's law). QED

Proposition 3.5. Under assumptions 2–5 and 7 an equilibrium is an optimum.

Proof. See the proof of proposition 3.6.

First-Best Solutions to the Inefficiency Problem

Competition usually leads to an inefficient allocation when nonexistence difficulties are ignored. In this section we examine two policy measures aimed at generating an efficient allocation and discuss their drawbacks.

VARIABLE INSURANCE PREMIUM POLICY

The inefficiency of equilibria stems from variable probability distributions. A straightforward solution would be to have a variable insurance premium to take into account heterogeneity of risks.

Proposition 3.6. If the variable insurance premium is defined by $q^s(x_1) = \pi^s(x_1)$, $s = 1, \ldots, S$, then under assumptions 1–5 there exists a competitive uniform strong equilibrium that sustains an efficient allocation.

Proof. A representative consumer faces the following program.

$$\text{Max } V(x) \tag{3.17}$$

subject to

$$x_1 - w_1 + \sum_{s=1}^{S} \pi^s(x_1)(x_2^s - w_2^s) \leq 0,$$

$$x_1 \geq 0, \quad x_2^s \geq 0, \qquad s = 1, \ldots, S.$$

This problem has a solution, since $V(x)$ is continuous and the feasible set is compact. Any such solution or any convex combination of such solutions is an efficient equilibrium. Let $[\Delta^*, (\lambda^{\delta*}), (x^{\delta*})]$ be such a convex combination of solutions to problem 3.17. Feasibility is obvious.

Assume now that there exists a better feasible allocation $[\Delta, (\lambda^\delta), (x^\delta)]$, that is, such that there exists $\delta' \in \Delta$ with $U(x^{\delta'}) > U(x^{\delta*})$ and $U(x^\delta) \geq U(x^{\delta*})$ for all other δ. By the feasibility constraint either

$$(x_1^\delta - w_1) + \sum_{s=1}^{S} \pi^s(x_1^\delta)(x_2^{s\delta} - w_2^s) \leqq 0 \quad \text{for all } \delta \in \Delta,$$

or there exists $\delta'' \in \Delta$ such that

$$(x_1^{\delta''} - w_1) + \sum_{s=1}^{S} \pi^s(x_1^{\delta''})(x_2^{s\delta''} - w_2^s) < 0.$$

In the first case x^δ is feasible for all $\delta \in \Delta$, so $U(x^\delta) \leqq U(x^{\delta*})$ for all $\delta \in \Delta$, a contradiction. In the second case $U(x^{\delta''}) < U(x^{\delta*})$ by assumption 4, a contradiction.   QED

The variable insurance premium policy generates an efficient allocation of resources because it makes every consumer "properly" account for the purchase of x_1—its impact not only on the probability distribution but also on resource gains resulting from redistribution of old consumers over the states of nature.

Of course, the difficulties of this policy are informational ones, and they are tremendous. The insurance company must know the form of the function $\pi^s(\cdot), s = 1, \ldots, S$, but it must also know the exact amount of x_1 bought by every individual.

TAXATION

The analogy with externalities suggests the possibility of taxation.

Assumption 8. $V(x)$ is strictly quasi-concave and differentiable.

Proposition 3.7. Under assumptions 1–5 and 8 there exists an efficient taxation scheme supporting the efficient allocation x^*, defined as

$$t_1 = \sum_{s=1}^{S} \frac{d\pi^s}{dx_1}\bigg|_{x_1 = x_1^*} (x_2^{s*} - w_2^s),$$

$$t_2^s = 0, \qquad s = 1, \ldots, S,$$

where t_1 is the taxation rate on consumption by young consumers and t_2^s is the taxation rate on consumption by old consumers in state s, for $s = 1, \ldots, S$.

Proof. The efficient allocation x^* is the solution of

$$\text{Max } V(x)$$

subject to

$$(x_1 - w_1) + \sum_{s=1}^{S} \pi^s(x_1)(x_2^s - w_2^s) \leq 0,$$

$$x \geq 0.$$

The first-order conditions that are necessary under assumption 8 are

$$\sum_{s=1}^{S} \left[\frac{d\pi^s(x_1)}{dx_1} U^s(x_1, x_2^s) + \pi^s(x_1) \frac{\partial U^s}{\partial x_1}(x_1, x_2^s) \right]$$

$$= \mu \left[1 + \sum_{s=1}^{S} \frac{d\pi^s(x_1)}{dx_1}(x_2^s - w_2^s) \right],$$

$$\pi^s(x_1) \frac{\partial U^s}{\partial x_2^s}(x_1, x_2^s) = \mu \pi^s(x_1), \qquad s = 1, \ldots, S.$$

On the other hand, the maximization problem of a consumer in an economy with taxation is

$$\text{Max } V(x)$$

subject to

$$x_1(1 + t_1) \leqq w_1 - \sum_{s=1}^{S} q^s z^s,$$

$$x_2^s(1 + t_2^s) \leqq w_2^s + z^s, \qquad s = 1, \ldots, S,$$

$$x \geqq 0. \tag{3.18}$$

The constraints (3.18) can be rewritten as

$$x_1(1 + t_1) + \sum_{s=1}^{S} q^s[(1 + t_2^s)x_2^s - w_2^s] \leq w_1,$$

$$x \geqq 0. \tag{3.19}$$

The first-order conditions are

$$\sum_{s=1}^{S} \left[\frac{d\pi^s(x_1)}{dx_1} U^s(x_1, x_2^s) + \pi^s(x_1) \frac{\partial U^s}{\partial x_1} (x_1, x_2^s) \right] = \mu(1 + t_1),$$

$$\pi^s(x_1) \frac{\partial U^s}{\partial x_2^s} (x_1, x_2^s) = \mu q^s(1 + t_2^s),$$

with perfect competition at the equilibrium $q^s = \pi^s(x_1)$. The identification of the two sets of first-order conditions leads to the result.   QED

This tax system has special features. Young consumers and old consumers pay different taxes, and if there were different types, each type would face its own tax scheme. The implicit assumption, then, is that the government is able and willing to tax different consumers differently.

When $V(x)$ is not quasi-concave, an efficient tax scheme may still exist (as it does in the example of the third section when an equilibrium exists), but in general it is not possible to support the set of preferred consumption bundles at the efficient point, even locally. Therefore nonconvexities often preclude the taxation solution. In the following example taxation is impossible.

Let

$$S = 2,$$
$$U^1(x_1, x_2^1) = x_2^1,$$
$$U^2(x_1, x_2^2) = 0,$$

$$\pi^1(x_1) = \frac{9}{(x_1 + 10)^2}, \qquad 0 \leqq x_1 \leqq 90,$$
$$= 9 \times 10^{-4}, \qquad x_1 \geqq 90,$$
$$w_1 = 10, \quad w_2^1 = 10, \quad w_2^2 = 106.$$
$$V(x) = \pi^1(x_1)x_2^1.$$

The optimum occurs for $x_1 = 2$, represented by point O_1 on the indifference curve of figure 3.3. Obviously this point cannot be globally supported, but it can be locally supported by a tax scheme. If $w_2^2 = \frac{106}{8} - 10$, then the optimum O_2 is obtained with $w_1 = 90$; it cannot be supported even locally.

Second-Best Solutions to the Inefficiency

The crucial step toward efficiency is the knowledge of the exact risk represented by a consumer. Each time a signal correlated with the consumption of a good in the first period is available, there is some hope for improving efficiency by connecting premiums to the information embodied in this signal. However, each problem requires its own analysis, and it seems that nothing general can be said about the cases in

Fig. 3.3

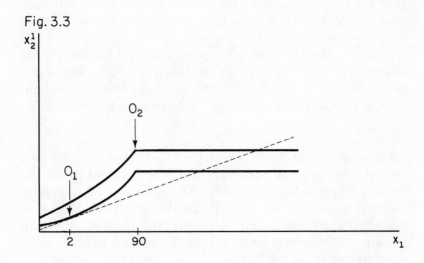

which the use of signals really leads to an improvement over the simple competitive outcome.

Appendix 3.A. The Generalized Expected Utility Hypothesis

Several papers in the economics of insurance (Ehrlich and Becker 1972, Pauly 1968), have introduced a generalized form of the expected utility hypothesis to formalize the behavior of consumers faced with uncertainty. In these formulations the Von Neumann utility functions depend on states of nature; but Hirshleifer (1970) and Arrow (1974) have shown that this generalization is consistent with Savage's approach (1954). In these papers the subjective probability distributions attached to the Von Neumann utility functions are supposed to depend on actions taken by agents. This feature seems to contradict Savage's requirement that the definition and the probability distribution of states of the world be independent of actions by agents.

This appendix shows that this formulation is consistent with the Savagian approach in the following sense. There is a way of defining genuine states of the world that are independent of actions; then Savage's theory may be used to construct a traditional Von Neumann utility function. The information specific to insurance problems then allows us to rewrite the expected utility function in a form identical to the one used by Hirshleifer (1970) and Arrow (1974). This interpretation has the further advantage of shedding some light on the nonconcavity difficulties inherent in these formulations.

Consider a consumer who lives two periods. In the first period there is no uncertainty, and in the second period he faces S different states of health. To each state of health is associated a level of income R^s. In the first period he may spend part of his income R^0 on preventive medical care in an attempt to influence his health in the second period, or he may save to consume in the next period. Let x^0 be the consumption in preventive medical care, let e be the savings in the first period, and let x^s be the consumption in state s of period 2, for $s = 1, \ldots, S$. The probability of being in state s in the second period with a consumption x^0 of preventive medical care in the first period is denoted $\pi^s(x^0)$, for $x = 1, \ldots, S$.

The optimization program of the consumer can then be written

$$\text{Max} \sum_{s=1}^{S} \pi^s(x^0) U^s(x^s)$$

subject to

$$x^0 + e = R^0,$$

$$x^s = R^s + e, \qquad s = 1, \ldots, S,$$
$$e, x^0 \geq 0, x^s \geq 0, \qquad s = 1, \ldots, S,$$

or

$$\text{Max} \sum_{s=1}^{S} \pi^s(x^0) U^s(R^s + R^0 - x^0)$$

subject to

$$R^0 \geq x^0 \geq 0.$$

The crucial point is to understand how agents can influence the probability distribution of their states of health. One interpretation is as follows.

Let ν be a description of all unalterable characteristics of the body relevant to health. Suppose that $\nu \in A$. Let $\mathcal{A}$ be a σ-algebra on A, and let $(A, \mathcal{A})$ be the fundamental (measurable) space of states of the world for the consumer.

The health of the consumer in period 2 depends on his unknown physical condition and on the preventive medical care he took in the first period according to medical technology

$$s = s(\nu, x^0) = s_{x^0}(\nu).$$

In Savage's language, x^0 is an act that maps the space of states of the world into the space of consequences, in this case $C = \tilde{S} \times R$, where a point in $\tilde{S} = \{1, \ldots, S\}$ defines the state of health and a point in R defines consumption; that is,

$$
\begin{aligned}
x^0(\cdot) &= s(\cdot, x^0) \\
&= x(\cdot, x^0).
\end{aligned}
$$

We restrict our attention to measurable acts.

From a well-known set of axioms (Savage 1954) we can deduce the existence of a probability measure P on $(A, \mathcal{A})$ and the existence of a Von Neumann utility function U such that the preordering of the consumer on the space of acts can be represented by the following expected utility.

$$
V(x^0) = \int_A U(s(\cdot, x^0), x(\cdot, x^0))dP(\cdot). \tag{3.20}
$$

We now use the special structure of the problem. Since the state of health is a sufficient statistic to define the income of a consumer, his consumption is constant for all states of the world leading to the same state of health:

$$
x(\nu, x^0) = x[s(\nu, x^0), x^0].
$$

Then

$$
x(\nu, x^0) = x(\nu', x^0) \quad \text{if } s(\nu, x^0) = s(\nu', x^0).
$$

Therefore equation 3.20 may be rewritten as

$$
\int_A U[s(\cdot, x^0), x(s(\cdot, x^0), x^0)]dP(\cdot) \tag{3.21}
$$

$$
= \sum_{s=1}^{S} U(s, x(s, x^0)) \int_{s_{x^0}^{-1}(s)} dP(\cdot), \tag{3.22}
$$

which is well defined since $s_{x^0}^{-1}(s) \in \mathcal{A}$.

Let $\pi^s(x^0) = \int_{s_{x^0}^{-1}(s)} dP(\cdot)$ and $U^s(x(s, x^0)) = U(s, x(s, x^0))$. Then 3.22 becomes

$$
\sum_{s=1}^{S} \pi^s(x^0)U(s, x(s, x^0)) \tag{3.24}
$$

$$= \sum_{s=1}^{S} \pi^s(x^0)U^s(R^s + R^0 - x^0), \qquad (3.25)$$

since $x(s, x^0) = R^s + R^0 - x^0$.

Now assume that s is a continuous real variable with values in a compact interval S. Then 3.20 must be written as

$$\int_S \pi^s(x^0)U^s(R^s + R^0 - x^0)ds. \qquad (3.26)$$

We want to use the form 3.21 to define a set of assumptions under which 3.26 is concave.

Assumption 9. The utility function $U(s, x)$ is concave and increasing in (s, x).

The requirement that U be increasing in s is easy to satisfy if utility increases with the quality of health and the quality of health is a unidimensional variable. If health were considered a multidimensional variable, more restrictions would be required. The concavity in s might be understood as the usual decreasing marginal utility property applied to health, but the qualitative nature of the variable s makes this interpretation dubious.

Assumption 10. The future health of the consumer $s(\cdot, x^0)$ is concave in x^0.

The same comment is relevant. It appears that assumptions 9 and 10 can be obtained separately by a redefinition of s, but they must hold simultaneously; together they correspond to a real constraint that says that the impact of x^0 on the (cardinal) Von Neumann utility through the intermediary of health has decreasing marginal returns.

Let $R(\nu, x^0) = R(s) + R^0 = R(s(\nu, x^0)) + R^0$.

Assumption 11. The consumer's income $R(\cdot, x^0)$ is concave in x^0.

The impact of preventive medical care on income must be decreasing marginal returns for any state of the world.

Lemma.   Under assumptions 9–11, $V(x^0)$ is concave.

Proof. V is a sum of increasing concave functions of concave functions.

In general it is very difficult to know whether these assumptions are satisfied, since medical technology is very complex. However, to obtain concavity of the expected utility, it is only necessary for consumers to believe that medical technology is as assumptions 9–11 describe.

In any case it is now possible to see intuitively why the function $V(x^0)$ may (or may not) be concave. It was very difficult to have any intuitive idea with the form 3.26.

4

Court against Moral Hazard

The basic function of law, in an economic perspective, is to alter incentives.

R. A. Posner (1972)

In an economy with insurance but moral hazard, the competitive equilibrium may fail to exist and is inefficient when it exists. The possible nonexistence of an equilibrium is somewhat surprising, since it seems that the use of a continuum of agents should overcome the difficulties created by the usual nonconcavity of the utility function that results from moral hazard. The inefficiency, which is independent of the nonconcavity, can be solved theoretically by using a nonlinear premium schedule related to the actions influencing the probabilities; however, this solution requires the ex ante monitoring of these actions, a task that is informationally very demanding and often impossible.

The purpose of this chapter is twofold. First we inquire whether the nonexistence question is important enough to justify the emergence of economic institutions or whether it is economically insignificant. Here we use a model that is a generalization of Pauly (1974). Even though the nonexistence question reappears, the lack of one insurance market is sufficient to yield an existence proof. Since the absence of insurance for the accident-free state is economically meaningful, the possible nonexistence of a competitive equilibrium in an economy with homogeneous agents and moral hazard and with a complete set of insurance markets is not a significant economic phenomenon. The absence of an insurance market might introduce an additional inefficiency, but in general it does not. The second purpose of this chapter is to explore a different solution to the inefficiency. Instead of monitoring ex ante the actions of the agents, we can trust the agents' declarations about these actions, establish an ex post control by a court, and tie the insurance payments to the outcome of negligence suits which attempt to establish the veracity of agents' initial declarations. With concavity assumptions an equilibrium exists, and it is usually but not always efficient.

Competitive Equilibrium

The economy is represented by a one-period model. There are two kinds of agents, consumers and insurance companies.

CONSUMERS

There is a continuum of identical agents (taken to be $[0, 1]$), who can be in S possible states (of health, for example). The "normal" state is state 1; states $s = 2, \ldots, S$ correspond to accidents. For simplicity, there is only one commodity in the economy and its price is normalized to 1. Let $w = (w^1, \ldots, w^S)$ be the vector of initial resources in the different states; then $w^s = w^1 - l^s$ where $l^s \geq 0$ is the loss due to accident $s, s = 2, \ldots, S$. This unique commodity can be used for direct consumption; alternatively, it can be used to modify the probabilities of the states. Let x^0 be the quantity used for the second purpose (often referred to as the level of care), and let $x = (x^1, \ldots, x^S)$ be the vector of direct consumption levels in the different states. Moreover, purchase of insurance is available for each possible accident $s = 2, \ldots, S$. Let $z^s \geq 0$ be the amount of insurance bought for state $s = 2, \ldots, S$, and let q^s be the price of one unit of insurance in state s. Then $q^s z^s$ is the premium associated with the insurance payment z^s in state s.

Assumption 1. The endowment $w^s > 0$, $s = 1, \ldots, S$. Let π^s be the probability that a consumer is in state s.

Assumption 2. The vector of probabilities $\pi = (\pi^1, \ldots, \pi^S)$ is a continuous function of $x^0 \in R_+$ with values in the simplex of R^S.

Assumption 3. Each consumer satisfies a generalized expected utility hypothesis. His utility function is

$$V(x) = \sum_{s=1}^{S} \pi^s(x^0) U^s(x^s),$$

with $U^s(\cdot)$ continuous and increasing, $s = 1, \ldots, S$.

The optimization program of a representative consumer[1] is then

$$\text{Max } V(x) \tag{4.1}$$

subject to

$$x^1 \leq w^1 - x^0 - \sum_{s'=2}^{S} q^{s'} z^{s'},$$

$$x^s \leq w^s - x^0 - \sum_{s'=2}^{S} q^{s'} z^{s'} + z^{s'}, \qquad s = 2, \ldots, S,$$

$$z^s \geq 0, \qquad\qquad\qquad s = 2, \ldots, S,$$
$$x^s \geq 0, \qquad\qquad\qquad s = 1, \ldots, S,$$
$$x^0 \geq 0.$$

Let $A(q)$ be the set of actions $a = (x^0, x^1, \ldots, x^S, z^2, \ldots, z^S)$ that are solutions to program 4.1, and let $\xi(q) = \varphi \circ A(q)$, be the set of vectors $(x^0, z^2, \ldots, z^S)$ obtained from $A(q)$ by projection.

Let

$$I^S = [\underline{\pi}^s, \overline{\pi}^s] = \left[\inf_{x^0 \geq 0} \pi^s(x^0), \sup_{x^0 \geq 0} \pi^s(x^0) \right],$$

---

1. It would be easy to generalize the results to several types of identical consumers.

and

$$Q = \prod_{s=1}^{S} I^S.$$

Assumption 4. $\pi^s > 0, s = 1, \ldots, S.$

INSURANCE COMPANIES

Insurance companies are not able to discriminate among consumers according to the amount of care the consumer does or does not take. They sell insurance in unrestricted amounts at prices $q^s, s = 2, \ldots, S$. Consider two different institutional arrangements.

Assumption 5.   There is perfect competition among insurance companies.

By this assumption, we mean not only that insurance companies are price takers but also that each company deals with a set of consumers with positive measure, so that probabilities are relevant for its maximization behavior.

Assumption 5'.   There exists a unique insurance company with an institutional zero-profit constraint on each type of contract.

EXISTENCE OF A COMPETITIVE EQUILIBRIUM

Since the solution of program 4.1 is not in general unique, identical consumers may have different behaviors. Let λ^δ be the measure of consumers taking actions $a^\delta = (x^{0\delta}, x^{1\delta}, \ldots, x^{S\delta}, z^{2\delta}, \ldots, z^{S\delta}).$

Definition.   A *competitive equilibrium* is a finite set Δ, a set of positive weights $\lambda^\delta, \delta \in \Delta$, adding to 1, a price vector $q^* \in Q$, a set of actions $a^{*\delta}$ such that

$$\sum_{\delta \in \Delta} \lambda^\delta q^{*s} z^{*s\delta} = \sum_{\delta \in \Delta} \lambda^\delta \pi^s(x^{*0\delta}) z^{*s\delta}, \qquad s = 2, \ldots, S, \quad (4.2)$$

$$\sum_{s=1}^{S} \sum_{\delta \in \Delta} \lambda^\delta \pi^s(x^{*0\delta}) x^{*s\delta} + \sum_{\delta \in \Delta} \lambda^\delta x^{*0\delta} = \sum_{s=1}^{S} \sum_{\delta \in \Delta} \lambda^\delta \pi^s(x^{*0\delta}) w^s, \quad (4.3)$$

$$a^{*\delta} \in A(q^*), \qquad \delta \in \Delta. \tag{4.4}$$

Equation 4.2 assures zero profit on each type of insurance contract, and 4.3 is the clearing condition for the market of the good. If Δ is reduced to a single element, the equilibrium is said to be uniform. When the equilibrium is not uniform, identical consumers face different risks due to different amounts of care x^0. Since insurance companies are not able to observe x^0, this is no problem. However, it creates an incentive for consumers to attempt to signal this difference. (See Rothschild and Stiglitz 1973 for an analysis of the induced adverse selection problems; under assumption 5' these difficulties do not arise.) Moreover, insurance companies might be tempted to use the signaling provided by different $z^{s\delta}$ to discriminate among consumers.

Theorem 4.1. Under assumptions 1–5 there exists a competitive equilibrium.[2]

Proof. In view of Green (1971, lemma 3–10) and Debreu (1959), the correspondence $\xi(q) = \varphi \circ A(q)$ is upper hemicontinuous from Q into a compact set with nonempty compact values.

Let

$$\Psi(q) = \{z^2, \ldots, z^S, \pi^2(x^0)z^2, \ldots, \pi^S(x^0)z^S\},$$

such that $(x^0, z^2, \ldots, z^S) \in \xi(q)$. Con $\Psi(\cdot)$ is then an upper hemicontinuous, nonempty, compact, convex-valued correspondence from Q into $R^{2(S-1)}$ (Hildenbrand 1974, proposition 6).

The expression $y \in$ con $\Psi(q)$ means

$$y = \sum_{\delta \in \Delta} \lambda^\delta [z^{2\delta}, \ldots, z^{S\delta}, \pi^2(x^{0\delta})z^{2\delta}, \ldots, \pi^S(x^{0\delta})z^{S\delta}],$$

---

2. Of course, to assure the existence of an equilibrium there is always the possibility of having very large prices of insurance so that nobody buys insurance. But we are interested in a fair system of insurance which would be optimal without moral hazard, hence the restriction to Q. Then the existence problem is no longer trivial.

where $(x^{0\delta}, z^{2\delta}, \ldots, z^{S\delta}) \in \xi(q)$ and where Δ is a finite set of $2S - 1$ elements at most by the Carathéodory theorem [$\Psi(Q)$ lies in the Euclidean space of dimension $2(S - 1)$] and where $\lambda^\delta > 0$ if $\delta \in \Delta$.

Now for $y \in R^{2S-2}$ consider the projection functions

$$P^s(y) = y^s, \qquad s = 1, \ldots, 2S - 2,$$

where y^s is the sth coordinate of y.

Note that for $y \in \text{con } \Psi(q)$,

$$P^{s-1}(y) = \sum_{\delta \in \Delta} \lambda^\delta z^{s\delta}, \qquad\qquad s = 2, \ldots, S,$$

$$P^{S-2+s}(y) = \sum_{\delta \in \Delta} \lambda^\delta \pi^s(x^{0\delta}) z^{s\delta}, \qquad s = 2, \ldots, S.$$

Then we construct the correspondence Γ from $\cup_{q \in Q} \text{con } \Psi(q)$ into Q defined as

$$q^s = \frac{P^{S-2+s}(y)}{P^s(y)}, \quad \text{if } P^s(y) \neq 0,$$

$$= [\underline{\pi}^s, \overline{\pi}^s], \quad \text{if } P^s(y) = 0.$$

For $y \in \text{con } \Psi(q)$,

$$q^s = \frac{\sum_{\delta \in \Delta} \lambda^\delta \pi^s(x^{0\delta}) z^{s\delta}}{\sum_{\delta \in \Delta} \lambda^\delta z^{s\delta}} \leqq \frac{\overline{\pi}^s \sum_{\delta \in \Delta} \lambda^\delta z^{s\delta}}{\sum_{\delta \in \Delta} \lambda^\delta z^{s\delta}} = \overline{\pi}^s.$$

Similarly,

$$q^s \geqq \underline{\pi}^s.$$

From Cellina (1969, theorem 2), we know that there exists $\hat{\Gamma}$, from $Z = $ closure of con $\cup_{q \in Q} \text{con } \Psi(q)$ into Q, which is upper hemicontinuous with compact, convex values and such that $\hat{\Gamma}(y) = \Gamma(y)$, for $y \in \cup_{q \in Q} \text{con } \Psi(q)$.

Let $\theta(q, y) = [\hat{\Gamma}(y), \text{con } \Psi(q)]$; it is an upper hemicontinuous correspondence with nonempty convex, compact values from the nonempty, convex, compact set $Q \times Z$ into itself. From the Kakutani theorem, $\theta(\cdot)$ has a fixed point (q^*, y^*) such that $y^* \in \text{con } \Psi(q^*)$.

If $P^s(y^*) = 0$, $s \in \{2, \ldots, S\}$, contract s makes zero profit, since nobody uses it. If $P^s(y^*) \neq 0$, contract s also makes zero profit, since $q^* \in \Gamma(y^*)$ implies

$$\sum_{\delta \in \Delta} \lambda^\delta \pi^s(x^{*0\delta}) z^{*s\delta} = q^{*s} \sum_{\delta \in \Delta} \lambda^\delta z^{*s\delta}.$$

By Walras's law, the market of the good is also cleared. QED

It is easy to avoid trivial equilibria where prices of insurance are so high that nobody buys insurance. In particular, if $\Sigma_{s=2}^S \overline{\pi}^s < 1$, it is clear that the agent will usually buy insurance. This is not to say that this is the right amount for efficiency. It is also easy to see that the nonexistence problem could appear here if we had S insurance contracts (instead of $S - 1$). In the construction of Γ there is no guaranty that the sum of the q^s is larger than or equal to one, but the range of the analog of $\Psi(q)$ could not have been restricted to a compact set. The example in which no equilibrium exists, given in chapter 3, can easily be adapted to this model.

Inefficiency of the Competitive Equilibrium

In general the competitive equilibrium is not efficient, for two reasons. First, the market of insurance for state 1 does not exist; second, with the competitive price q^* consumers do not properly take into account the impact of their consumption x^0 on the technology of insurance companies; if all consumers were more careful, the fair price of insurance would be lower.

Why does the first inefficiency not usually occur? Consider the program that yields the Pareto optimum, assumed to be unique for simplicity:

$$\text{Max } \pi^1(x^0)U^1(x^1) + \sum_{s=2}^S \pi^s(x^0)U^s(x^s), \qquad (4.5)$$

subject to

$$\sum_{s=1}^S \pi^s(x^0)x^s + x^0 = \sum_{s=1}^S \pi^s(x^0)w^s,$$

$$x^s \geqq 0, \qquad s = 0, 1, \ldots, S. \qquad (4.6)$$

At the optimum there exists a state s toward which no transfer of purchasing power is realized. Consider the state from which the most purchasing power comes, the one for which $w^s - x^{0*} - x^{s*}$ has the largest positive value. Call this state 1. (The optimum is denoted by stars.)

Suppose now that instead of price q, insurance companies offer premium schedules $\pi(x^0)$ depending on the amount of care. The program of a consumer is

$$\text{Max } \pi^1(x^0)U^1(x^1) + \sum_{s=2}^{S} \pi^s(x^0)U^s(x^s), \tag{4.7}$$

subject to

$$x^1 = w^1 - x^0 - \sum_{s=2}^{S} \pi^s(x^0)z^s, \tag{4.8}$$

$$x^s = w^s - x^0 + z^s - \sum_{s=2}^{S} \pi^s(x^0)z^s, \qquad s = 2, \ldots, S,$$

$$x^0 \geqq 0$$
$$x^s \geqq 0, \qquad\qquad\qquad\qquad\qquad s = 1, \ldots, S,$$
$$z^s \geqq 0, \qquad\qquad\qquad\qquad\qquad s = 2, \ldots, S.$$

With such a program we can reach the optimum of the consumer choice problem given in 4.5 and 4.6.

Choose

$$x^0 = x^{*0}, \qquad z^1 = 0,$$
$$z^s = (w^1 - x^{*0} - x^{*1}) - (w^s - x^{*0} - x^{*s}), \qquad s = 2, \ldots, S;$$

by definition

$$z^s \geqq 0, \qquad\qquad\qquad\qquad\qquad s = 1, \ldots, S,$$

$$z^s - \sum_{s=2}^{S} \pi^s(x^{*0})z^s = x^{*s} + x^{*0} - w^s, \qquad s = 2, \ldots, S.$$

Then with the premium schedule $\pi(\cdot)$ it is possible to achieve a Pareto optimum. In this case the lack of insurance for state 1 does not create an inefficiency.

Assumption 6.   The transfer of a good allowed by the non-existent insurance market would not be used at the Pareto optimum.[3]

Assumption 6 is economically very reasonable, since the accident-free state is a natural candidate, and it suggests that with this choice of the missing market, the first inefficiency of the competitive equilibrium will not occur. However, the moral hazard inefficiency may drive the economy toward a region where the market to which no transfer is wished changes.

The moral hazard inefficiency can easily be seen under the assumption of concavity of the expected utility function $V(\cdot)$. Then the competitive equilibrium price is such that $q^* = \pi(x^{*0})$. The solution of program 4.1 is included in the feasible set of program 4.5. That it is strictly included can be checked with examples, as in chapter 3.

The solution of a nonlinear insurance premium related to the true level of care yields efficiency but is very costly in terms of information. There is another institutional arrangement that also achieves Pareto optimality and which we hope demands less information.

Introducing a Court as an Economic Agent

When consumers buy insurance against $S - 1$ accidents, the insurance company computes premiums according to the declared amount of care $\tilde{x}^0$. When an accident occurs, the insurance company asks a court to determine whether the declared amount of care was taken. With a probability of error depending on the difference between the true amount of care x^0 and the declared amount $\tilde{x}^0$, the court determines whether the consumer is guilty of negligence. If he is guilty, the insurance company does not make the payment.

3. Therefore the optimum constrained by the lack of this "market" remains a Pareto optimum.

If the court were infallible (discovered the true value of x^0 with probability one), the outcome of such an economy would be Pareto optimal (see theorem 4.3). The relevant problem would then be to compare the informational costs of discovering the true x^0 ex ante (to implement the solution suggested in the third section) and the transaction costs involved in using the court to rule on the consumers having accidents. However, it is plain that we cannot expect the court to be perfect.

Definitions. The *court* is characterized by the probability $\Psi(x^0 - \tilde{x}^0)$ with which an agent is declared not guilty. The court is *infallible* if $\Psi(y) = 1$ for $y \geq 0$, and $\Psi(y) = 0$ for $y < 0$.

Assumption 7. (a) The probability $\Psi(\cdot)$ is a continuous function from R into $[0, 1]$. (b) Moreover $\Psi(\cdot)$ is bounded below by a positive number on $[-w^1, w^1]$.

Assumption 8. The probability $\pi^s(\cdot)$ is decreasing in x^0, $s = 2, \ldots, S$.

The insurance company proposes to a consumer a premium schedule $\tilde{\pi}(\tilde{x}^0)$ that depends on the amount of care declared by him. Then we must determine whether an equilibrium premium schedule exists and what its form is.

The optimization program of a representative consumer is

$$\text{Max } \pi^1(x^0)U^1(x^1) + \sum_{s=2}^{S} \pi^s(x^0)[\Psi(x^0 - \tilde{x}^0)U^s(x^s)$$

$$+ (1 - \Psi(x^0 - \tilde{x}^0))U^s(x^s - z^s)], \quad (4.9)$$

subject to

$$x^1 = w^1 - x^0 - \sum_{s=2}^{S} \tilde{\pi}^s(\tilde{x}^0)z^s, \quad (4.10)$$

$$x^s = w^s - x^0 + z^s - \sum_{s=2}^{S} \tilde{\pi}^s(\tilde{x}^0)z^s, \qquad s = 2, \ldots, S,$$

$$x^0 \geqq 0,$$
$$x^s \geqq 0, \qquad\qquad\qquad\qquad s = 1, \ldots, S,$$
$$z^s \geqq 0, \qquad\qquad\qquad\qquad s = 2, \ldots, S,$$
$$\tilde{x}^0 \in [0, w^1]. \qquad\qquad\qquad\qquad\qquad\qquad (4.11)$$

This program is subject to the last constraint $\tilde{x}^0 \in [0, w^1]$ because the insurance company knows w^1 and because $\tilde{x}^0$ has to be credible.

Substituting the constraints 4.10 into the utility function, we have

$$\text{Max } V(x^0, \tilde{x}^0, z^2, \ldots, z^s, \tilde{\pi}(\cdot)), \qquad (4.12)$$

subject to

$$z^s \geqq 0, \qquad s = 2, \ldots, S,$$
$$x^0 \geqq 0,$$
$$w^1 \geqq \tilde{x}^0 \geqq 0,$$

$$w^1 - x^0 - \sum_{s=2}^{S} \tilde{\pi}^s(\tilde{x}^0)z^s \geqq 0,$$

$$w^s - x^0 + z^s - \sum_{s=2}^{S} \tilde{\pi}^s(\tilde{x}^0)z^s \geqq 0, \qquad s = 2, \ldots, S.$$

We first restrict $\tilde{\pi}(\cdot)$ to the set Δ of continuous functions from $[0^1, w^1]$ into $B = [0, 1]^{S-1}$, endowed with the uniform topology.

If all consumers have the same behavior, we know that at the equilibrium, the zero-profit condition on each contract implies $\tilde{\pi}(\tilde{x}^{*0}) = \pi(x^{*0})\Psi(x^{*0} - \tilde{x}^{*0})$. We then restrict our search for equilibrium premium schedules to the subfamily $D \subset \Delta$ indexed by k and k':

$$\tilde{\pi}^{skk'}(\tilde{x}^0) = \frac{\pi^s(k)}{\pi^s(k')}\, \pi^s(\tilde{x}^0)\Psi(k - \tilde{x}^0),$$

with

$$0 \leqq k \leqq w^1, \qquad 0 \leqq k' \leqq w^1.$$

Definition. A *court equilibrium* is an action vector $a^* = (x^{*0}, \tilde{x}^{*0}, x^{*1}, \ldots, x^{*S}, z^{*2}, \ldots, z^{*S})$ and a premium schedule $\tilde{\pi}^*(\cdot)$ such that

$$a^* \text{ is a solution of problem 4.12,} \qquad (4.13)$$

$$\tilde{\pi}^{*s}(\tilde{x}^{*0}) = \pi^s(x^{*0})\Psi(x^{*0} - \tilde{x}^{*0}),$$
$$\text{if } z^{*s} > 0, \qquad s = 2, \ldots, S, \quad (4.14)$$

$$x^{*0} + \sum_{s=1}^{S} \pi^s(x^{*0})(x^{*s} - w^s) = 0. \qquad (4.15)$$

Lemma 1. The function of (k, k'), $\tilde{\pi}^{kk'}(\cdot)$ is continuous from $[0, w^1] \times [0, w^1]$ into Δ under assumptions 2–4.

Proof. Let

$$\alpha^s(k, k', \tilde{x}^0) = \frac{\pi^s(k)}{\pi^s(k')} \cdot \pi^s(\tilde{x}^0) \cdot \Psi(k - \tilde{x}^0), \qquad s = 2, \ldots, S,$$

be a continuous function on the compact set $[0, w^1]^3$; then $\alpha = (\alpha^2, \ldots, \alpha^S)$ is uniformly continuous and in particular $\forall \epsilon > 0, \exists \eta > 0, \exists \eta' > 0, \forall k^0, k'^0$, such that

$$|k - k^0| < \eta, \qquad |k' - k'^0| < \eta',$$

implies

$$\sup_{x^0 \in [0, w^1]} \|\alpha(k, k', \tilde{x}^0) - \alpha(k^0, k'^0, \tilde{x}^0)\| < \epsilon,$$

which establishes the continuity of the function $(k, k') \rightarrow \alpha(k, k', \cdot)$ at k^0, k'^0.   QED

Lemma 2. D is a compact subspace of Δ, under assumptions 2–4.

Proof. From lemma 1, D is the image of the compact set $[0, w^1] \times [0, w^1]$ by a continuous function.   QED

Assumption 9. The solution of program 4.9 is single valued.[4]

---

4. This assumption replaces an assumption of concavity on the objective function and the feasible set in program 4.9.

Theorem 4.2. Under assumptions 1–4 and 7–9 there exists a court equilibrium.

Proof. From assumptions 4 and 7 any $\tilde{\pi}(\cdot) \in D$, as a function of $\tilde{x}^0$, is uniformly bounded below by a positive number.

Since the uniform convergence is finer than the compact open topology (Kelley 1970), the objective function and the constraint correspondence of program 4.12 are continuous in $\tilde{\pi}(\cdot)$. Therefore by the maximum theorem and assumption 9 the action correspondence $A(\cdot)$ is a continuous function from D into R^{2S+1}.

Let Γ be the continuous function that associates to the action the function

$$\frac{\pi^s(x^0)}{\pi^s(\tilde{x}^0)} \cdot \pi^s(\cdot) \cdot \Psi(x^0 - \cdot), \qquad s = 2, \ldots, S.$$

Let Φ be the function from D to D, $\Phi = \Gamma{\circ}A$. From the Schauder-Tychonoff theorem $\Phi(\cdot)$ has a fixed point. One can easily verify that it is a court equilibrium. QED

Assumption 10. $\Sigma_{s=2}^{S}[\pi^s(y^1)/\pi^s(y^2)]\pi^s(y^3) < 1$, $\forall(y^1, y^2, y^3) \in [0, w^1]^3$.
For all $s = 2, \ldots, S$,

$$\frac{d^+U^s(w^s - x^0)}{dx^s} > \frac{d^+U^s(w^1 - x^0)}{dx^1}, \qquad \forall x^0 \in [0, w^1],$$

where d^+/d denotes the right derivative, which is assumed to exist.

Theorem 4.3. Under assumptions 2, 6, 8, and 10, with an infallible court, equilibria are efficient.

Proof. Consider an equilibrium such that $\tilde{x}^{*0} > x^{*0}$. For any $\tilde{x}^0 > x^{*0}$, $\tilde{\pi}^s(\tilde{x}^0) = 0$, $s = 2, \ldots, S$. Any $(z^2, \ldots, z^S)$ and any $\tilde{x}^0 > x^{*0}$, associated with $(x^{*0}, x^{*1}, \ldots, x^{*S})$ solution of the program 4.16 form a solution 4.9 under $\tilde{x}^0 > x^{*0}$.

$$\text{Max } \pi^1(x^0)U^1(x^1) + \sum_{s=2}^{S} \pi^s(x^0)U^s(x^s), \qquad (4.16)$$

subject to

$$x^s = w^s - x^0, \qquad s = 1, \ldots, S,$$
$$0 \leqq x^0 \leqq w^s, \qquad s = 1, \ldots, S.$$

Consider $\tilde{x}^0 \leqq x^{*0}$; the agent can then achieve a level of utility defined by the program

$$\text{Max } \pi^1(x^0)U^1(x^1) + \sum_{s'=2}^{S} \pi^{s'}(x^0)U^{s'}(x^{s'}),$$

subject to

$$x^1 = w^1 - x^0 - \sum_{s'=2}^{S} \frac{\pi^{s'}(x^{*0})}{\pi^{s'}(\tilde{x}^{*0})} \cdot \pi^{s'}(\tilde{x}^0)z^{s'},$$

$$x^s = w^s - x^0 + z^s - \sum_{s'=2}^{S} \frac{\pi^{s'}(x^{*0})}{\pi^{s'}(\tilde{x}^{*0})} \cdot \pi^{s'}(\tilde{x}^0)z^{s'}, \qquad s = 2, \ldots, S,$$

$$x^0 \geqq 0,$$
$$x^s \geqq 0, \qquad s = 1, \ldots, S, \, 0 \leqq \tilde{x}^0 \leqq w^1,$$
$$z^s \geqq 0, \qquad s = 2, \ldots, S.$$

Clearly, the agent would lose some consumption by putting $\tilde{x}^0$ strictly less than x^0 (assumption 8) and would gain nothing. Therefore he puts $\tilde{x}^0 = x^0$.
His behavior is then the solution of

$$\text{Max } \pi^1(x^0)U^1(x^0) + \sum_{s=2}^{S} \pi^s(x^0)U^s(x^s) \qquad (4.17)$$

subject to

$$x^1 = w^1 - x^0 - \sum_{s'=2}^{S} \frac{\pi^{s'}(x^{*0})}{\pi^{s'}(\tilde{x}^{*0})} \cdot \pi^{s'}(x^0)z^{s'},$$

$$x^s = w^s - x^0 + z^s - \sum_{s'=2}^{S} \frac{\pi^{s'}(x^{*0})}{\pi^{s'}(\tilde{x}^{*0})} \cdot \pi^{s'}(x^0)z^{s'}, \qquad s = 2, \ldots, S,$$

$$x^0 \geqq 0,$$
$$x^s \geqq 0, \qquad s = 1, \ldots, S,$$
$$z^s \geqq 0, \qquad s = 2, \ldots, S.$$

From assumption 10 the utility obtained through (4.17), is

larger than the utility obtained through 4.16. Therefore an equilibrium such that $\tilde{x}^{*0} > x^{*0}$ cannot occur.[5]

Now consider an equilibrium with $\tilde{x}^{*0} \leqq x^{*0}$. The same reasoning eliminates the cases with $\tilde{x}^{*0} < x^{*0}$. The only possible equilibria occur when $\tilde{x}^{*0} = x^{*0}$.

Then the agent solves the program

$$\text{Max } \pi^1(x^0)U^1(x^1) + \sum_{s'=2}^{S} \pi^{s'}(x^0)U^{s'}(x^{s'}) \qquad (4.18)$$

subject to

$$x^1 = w^1 - x^0 - \sum_{s'=2}^{S} \pi^{s'}(x^0)z^{s'},$$

$$x^s = w^s - x^0 + z^s - \sum_{s'=2}^{S} \pi^{s'}(x^0)z^{s'}, \qquad s = 2, \ldots, S,$$

$$x^0 \geqq 0,$$
$$x^s \geqq 0, \qquad s = 1, \ldots, S,$$
$$z^s \geqq 0, \qquad s = 2, \ldots, S.$$

From the third section and assumption 6, the equilibrium is efficient.   QED

Note that efficiency with the infallible court was obtained with the chosen family of premium schedules but would not be achieved in general with any continuous function. It is important for $\tilde{\pi}^s(\tilde{x}^0)$ to be related to $\pi^s(x^0)$ in order for agents to take into account the influence of self-protection.

There is still a difficulty in proving a continuity theorem at the infallible court Ψ^0, because the price of insurance goes to zero when the probability of being caught lying goes to one. The assumption 7b is no longer satisfied.

To solve this technical problem, we use the following assumption.

5. Without assumption 10 the solutions to 4.16 and 4.17 could lead to the same value of the objective function. Then the economy might well be stopped at an inefficient equilibrium, because of the very pessimistic initial expectations of insurers. However, competition among insurance companies should eliminate this inefficiency.

Assumption 11. The utility function $U^s(\cdot)$ is satiated for x^s very large, $x^s > w^s + w^1$, $s = 2, \ldots, S$.

Consider the space F of continuous functions on $\{[-w^1, w^1] - \{0\}\}$ with values in $[0, 1]$ endowed with the compact open topology.

Let A be the space of continuous functions on $[-w^1, w^1]$ with values in $[0, 1]$, and let $B = A \cup \Psi^0$; $B \subset F$ is endowed with the topology induced by the topology on F.

Theorem 4.4 Under assumptions 1–7a, 8, and 11 the court equilibrium action correspondence A, which associates to a court the equilibrium action vector, is upper hemicontinuous on B.

Proof. The only difficulty arises in the interesting case in which a sequence of courts Ψ^n converges to the infallible court Ψ^0 in the compact open topology. From theorem 4.2 and assumption 11, the equilibrium correspondence is never empty.

Since Ψ^n converges to Ψ^0 in the compact open topology, $V(\cdot)$ is a continuous function of Ψ^n; the correspondence defining the constraints is continuous in Ψ^n. The action correspondence $a(\cdot)$ is therefore continuous in Ψ^n by the maximum theorem. Consider then the sequence of equilibria a^n converging to a^0 associated with the sequence of courts Ψ^n: $a^n \in a(\Psi^n)$ implies $a^0 \in a(\Psi^0)$. Therefore a^0 is an equilibrium for Ψ^0, since the insurance contracts are balanced by continuity.

Consequently, A is a closed-graph correspondence. By assumption 11 the actions remain in a compact set (see program 4.18). Therefore $A(\cdot)$ is upper hemicontinuous.   QED

PART III

The Theory of First-Order Certainty Equivalence with Instrument-Dependent Randomness

The solution of maximization problems should satisfy two opposing requirements. First, it should be as exact as possible; second, it should be easy to obtain. This is true not only for operational research purposes but more fundamentally for giving credibility to the theory of the homo economicus.

Neoclassical economic theory describes its agents as maximizers of objective functions. When the solution of these maximization problems requires the most sophisticated results of dynamic programming under uncertainty with learning, however, the descriptive power of such a theory becomes very weak. A fundamental problem of economic theory is then to investigate the world of bounded rationality, in particular to characterize problems for which simple second-best solutions approximate first-best solutions, for which a normative theory is easier to develop. Then we can increase the credibility of the descriptive model without losing the relevance of an approximate normative theory.

It is in this spirit that we survey the theory of certainty and first-order certainty equivalence. We are given a maximization problem under uncertainty. The variables with respect to which the decision maker maximizes are called instruments, or control variables. These instruments, in conjunction with random variables and through a model, determine the values of uncontrolled variables that enter the decision maker's objective function as arguments. Without being very precise here, let us say that certainty equivalence holds when the solution of the stochastic maximization problem is identical to the solution of an associated certain problem in which random variables have been replaced by their expected values. This second problem is obviously much simpler to solve, so it is a perfect case in which there is a simple method for solving an apparently difficult maximization problem under uncertainty. Theil and Simon have obtained theorems that justify the use of certainty equivalents. Unfortunately, the range of problems for which certainty equivalence holds is very limited. We must then look for approximate certainty equivalence. Theil and Malinvaud have developed a theory of first-order certainty equivalence. Roughly speaking, first-order certainty equivalence holds when the solution of the stochastic maximization problem is equal to the first order to the solution of an associated certain problem, when uncertainty is small. A loss is incurred by such an approximation, but the loss is reasonably small when uncertainty itself is small. In a dynamic setting constraints on instruments of the first period are allowed. On the contrary, constraints on instruments in future periods may lead to a breakdown to the validity of certainty equivalents. A special case of this important point has received extensive attention in the discussion about the irreversibility of investment. The theory developed by Theil and Malinvaud is based on the assumption that the random variables of the problem are independent of instruments. However, in macroeconomics as well as in microeconomics, examples of instrument-dependent randomness are extremely numerous, and we ask under what conditions this instrument effect does not disturb the first-order certainty equivalence property. We discuss some economic applications of the results and extend the concept of first-order equivalence itself.

5

Certainty and First-Order Certainty Equivalence

Certainty Equivalence

Theil (1954) provided the first formalization of the intuitive concept of certainty equivalence in a framework of macroeconomic policy. His main result is based on the following assumptions.

Assumption 1. The decision maker's uncontrolled variables y are real-valued variables, and they are connected with his instruments x by the model 5.1, where g is a column vector of functions and e a column vector of random variables. The mean value of e is zero for any x, $Ee = 0$, and its covariance matrix Eee' is finite and independent of x.

$$y = g(x) + e,$$

where $x \in R^n$, and e (and consequently y) are random variables with values in R^m.

Assumption 2. All vectors x, y of instruments and uncontrolled variables are completely ordered according to the decision maker's preference in a way that allows a representation by means of the real-valued payoff function 5.2, where

$A(x)$ and $A_i(x)$ are independent of y and A_{ij} is independent of both x and y for $i = 1, \ldots, m$ and $j = 1, \ldots, m$.

$$U(x, y) = A(x) + \sum_{i=1}^{m} A_i(x)y_i + \frac{1}{2} \sum_{i=1}^{m} \sum_{j=1}^{m} A_{ij}y_i y_j. \qquad (5.2)$$

Theorem 5.1 (Theil 1954).   Under assumptions 1 and 2 maximization of the payoff function subject to the nonstochastic constraint $y = g(x)$, where the random vector e is replaced by its expected value, gives the same set of instrument vectors as maximization of the expected value of the payoff function subject to 5.1, provided that such a maximum exists.

Proof

$$EU(x, g(x) + e) = A(x) + \sum_{i=1}^{m} A_i(x)(g_i(x) + Ee_i)$$

$$+ \frac{1}{2} \sum_{i=1}^{m} \sum_{j=1}^{m} A_{ij}[g_i(x)g_j(x) + g_i(x)Ee_i$$

$$+ g_j(x)Ee_j + Ee_i e_j]$$

$$= A(x) + \sum_{i=1}^{m} A_i(x)g_i(x)$$

$$+ \frac{1}{2} \sum_{i=1}^{m} \sum_{j=1}^{m} [A_{ij}g_i(x)g_j(x) + Ee_i e_j]$$

$$= U(x, g(x)) + \frac{1}{2} \sum_{i=1}^{m} \sum_{j=1}^{m} A_{ij}Ee_i e_j$$

$$= U(x, g(x)) + C. \qquad (5.3)$$

Under the assumptions of the theorem, C is independent of x.[1] Therefore the objective function of the stochastic

1. Observe that if the matrix of variances and covariances of the random variables depend on the instruments, then C depends on x and the result breaks down. This question is considered in chapter 6.

problem, $EU(x, g(x) + e)$ and the objective function of the associated riskless problem, $U(x, g(x) + Ee) = U(x, g(x))$ differ only by a constant. Therefore the maximizers of the two problems are identical. QED

The result is believed to be less general than it actually is, because Theil used it essentially in the so-called linear quadratic case, that is, with a linear model

$$y = Rx + e, \quad \text{where } R \text{ is an } m \times n \text{ matrix}, \quad (5.4)$$

and with a quadratic payoff function

$$U(x, y) = y'Ay + x'Bx + y'Cx + K'x + P'y. \quad (5.5)$$

Theil (1958, 1964) applied this model to many different problems—problems in the theory of the consumer, the theory of the firm, and the theory of macroeconomic policy in the tradition of Tinbergen (1952).

It is often the case that the control variables are constrained. Let us assume that x must belong to a subset S of R^n. We immediately have the following theorem.

Theorem 5.2.   Theorem 5.1 still holds if, in addition, x is constrained to belong to a subset of R^n.

The notion of certainty equivalence in the static model is straightforward. We consider now a dynamic maximization problem under uncertainty in which information increases with time.

We formalize the increase of information in the following way. We have T periods. The randomness is represented by a set of T random variables $e_1, \ldots, e_T$. At date 1 all the variables $e_1, \ldots, e_T$ are random for the decision maker. At date 2 he knows the value taken by the random variable e_1, and the variables $e_2, \ldots, e_T$ are still random for him. He maximizes his expected utility using the conditional distributions of $e_2, \ldots, e_T$ given $e_1 \ldots$.

Let $x_t = (x_1(t), \ldots, x_n(t))$, $y_t = (y_1(t), \ldots, y_m(t))$ be, respectively, the vector of instruments and the vector of uncontrolled variables at date t. Let

$$x = \begin{bmatrix} x_1 \\ \cdot \\ \cdot \\ \cdot \\ x_T \end{bmatrix}, \quad y = \begin{bmatrix} y_1 \\ \cdot \\ \cdot \\ \cdot \\ y_T \end{bmatrix}, \quad e = \begin{bmatrix} e_1 \\ \cdot \\ \cdot \\ \cdot \\ e_T \end{bmatrix}.$$

With these definitions the payoff function can be written as before:

$$U(x, y) = y'Ay + x'Bx + y'Cx + K'x + P'y. \qquad (5.6)$$

The model is

$$y = Rx + e, \qquad Ee = 0, \qquad (5.7)$$

with

$$R = \begin{bmatrix} R_{11} & 0 & \cdots & & 0 \\ R_{21} & R_{22} & 0 & \cdots & 0 \\ \cdot & & & & \\ \cdot & & & & \\ \cdot & & & & \\ R_{T1} & R_{T2} & \cdots & & R_{TT} \end{bmatrix},$$

since we assume that the instruments of date t can influence only the uncontrolled variables of date t', $t' \geq t$.

Let $\tilde{x}$ be a strategy for this dynamic programming problem, where

$$\tilde{x} = \begin{bmatrix} x_1 \\ x_2(e_1) \\ \cdot \\ \cdot \\ \cdot \\ x_T(e_1, \ldots, e_{T-1}) \end{bmatrix}$$

We say that certainty equivalence holds if x_1 is equal to the optimal value of the first-period instrument in the certain problem where e is replaced by $Ee = 0$. Note that at period 1, x_1 is the only instrument that must be determined.

Theorem 5.3 (Theil 1957).   If the payoff is quadratic, if the relations between instruments and results are linear and stochastic only by additive random disturbances, if these disturbances have zero expectations and are independent of the instruments, if no loss of information occurs in the dynamic model, then certainty equivalence holds for the first-period decision of the sequential strategy, provided that a maximum exists.[2]

The proof is immediate since optimal future instruments at date t are linear forms over random variables of date $t' < t$. Substituting these instruments in the first-period objective function yields a problem of the type studied in theorem 5.1. However, this result requires more assumptions than theorem 5.1, as noted by Theil: "The reason for the additional restrictions in the dynamic model is that future measures are random within the framework of a strategy, and in that respect they are no different from the non-controlled variables."

As in theorem 5.2, constraints on instruments of the first period do not change the results. However, as observed by Sandee, constraints on instruments in future periods may lead to the breakdown of the certainty equivalence result.

Theorem 5.4.   When binding constraints on future values of instruments exist, even under the assumptions of theorem 5.3, certainty equivalence does not generally hold.

Proof.   The proof is obtained by constructing a counterexample.[3]

$$\underset{(x_1, x_2)}{\text{Max}} \; - y_1^2 - y_2^2 \tag{5.8}$$

2. Simon's analysis (1956) is a special case of this model for an inventory problem.

3. This example is due to Sandee. See footnote 8 in Malinvaud (1969b).

subject to

$$y_1 = x_1 + e_1,$$
$$y_2 = x_1 + x_2 + e_1,$$
$$x_2 \geqq 0,$$

where e_1 is a random variable that takes the value $-\epsilon$ with probability $\frac{2}{3}$ and the value 2ϵ with probability $\frac{1}{3}$. Therefore $Ee_1 = 0$ and Var $e_1 = 2\epsilon^2$.

We are in the framework of theorem 5.3, with the constraint $x_2 \geqq 0$ on the instrument of the second period.

The maximum of the riskless program associated with 5.8 is obtained for

$$\bar{x}_1 = 0, \qquad \bar{x}_2 = 0. \tag{5.9}$$

Now consider the stochastic program that is solved using a backward dynamic programming method. At the second period the agent knows the value of e_1; if $e_1 = -\epsilon$, then $x_2 = \max(0, -x_1 + \epsilon)$; if $e_1 = 2\epsilon$, then $x_2 = \max(0, -x_1 - 2\epsilon)$.

We consider three cases according to the value chosen for x_1.

Case 1: $x_1 \geqq \epsilon$. Then $x_2^* = 0$ in both cases and the objective function of the first period becomes

$$-2E(x_1 + e_1)^2; \tag{5.10}$$

hence $x_1^* = 0$ and $U^* = -4\epsilon^2$.

Case 2: $\epsilon > x_1 > -2\epsilon$. Then, $x_2^* = \epsilon - x_1$ if $e_1 = -\epsilon$, and $x_2^* = 0$ if $e_1 = 2\epsilon$. The objective function of the first period is

$$-E(x_1 + e_1)^2 - \tfrac{1}{3}(x_1 + 2\epsilon)^2; \tag{5.11}$$

hence $x_1^* = -\epsilon/2$ and $U^* = -3\epsilon^2$.

Case 3: $x_1 \leqq -2\epsilon$. Then $x_2^* = \epsilon - x_1$ if $e_1 = -\epsilon$, and $x_2^* = -x_1 - 2\epsilon$ if $e_1 = 2\epsilon$. The objective function of the first period is

$$-E(x_1 + e_1)^2; \tag{5.12}$$

hence $x_1^* = -2\epsilon$ and $U^* = -6\epsilon^2$.

The global optimum is therefore obtained with $x_1^* = -\epsilon/2$. Clearly $x_1^* \neq \bar{x}_1$. QED

Intuitively, the reason for the breakdown of certainty equivalence is the following. In theorem 5.3 the dynamic problem was reduced to a static problem by showing that future instruments are linear forms of past random variables. Because of the constraints, this result does not hold (see proof of theorem 5.4), and the essential linear quadratic structure disappears.

The limitations of the certainty equivalence results are obvious. We shall define an approximate certainty equivalence that holds with more general models and payoff functions.

First-Order Certainty Equivalence

Theil (1958, p. 72) introduced the concept of first-order certainty equivalence in the linear quadratic case with random parameters, but it was Malinvaud (1969a, 1969b) who provided a thorough discussion of the concept and extensions. We present first-order certainty equivalence in Malinvaud's framework.

The static model is now written

$$y_j = g_j(x_1, \ldots, x_n; e), \qquad j = 1, \ldots, m, \qquad (5.13)$$

or

$$y = g(x, e).$$

The joint probability distribution $f(e)$ of e (with values in R^p) is known, and $Ee = 0$. The payoff function is

$$U(x, y, e) = U(x, g(x, e), e). \qquad (5.14)$$

The optimization problem of the decision maker is

$$\operatorname*{Max}_x \int_{R^p} U(x, g(x, e), e)f(e)de. \qquad (5.15)$$

We associate with this stochastic problem a certain problem. However, several certain problems are possible, and therefore an ambiguity exists in the definition of the certainty equivalent (which is the solution of the certainty problem).

One simple way of defining certainty equivalence is to replace the random variables e by their expected values. The certainty problem then becomes

$$\underset{x}{\text{Max}} \ U(x, g(x, 0), 0). \qquad (5.16)$$

We introduce a small degree of randomness around this certainty situation by defining the positive parameter ϵ and the random variables ϵe where ϵ is small.[4]

Now consider the general maximization problem:

$$\underset{x}{\text{Max}} \int_{R^p} U(x, g(x, \epsilon e), \epsilon e) f(e) de. \qquad (5.17)$$

If $\epsilon = 1$, then 5.17 becomes 5.14; if $\epsilon = 0$, then 5.17 becomes 5.16.

First-order certainty equivalence holds if the solution of 5.17 is the same to the first order as the solution of 5.17 when ϵ is in the neighborhood of zero. It is then possible to use the solution of 5.16 to approximate the solution of 5.17.

However, Malinvaud (1969a) prefers another associated certain problem defined as follows. Let

$$\gamma_j(x, e) = g_j(x, e) - Eg_j(x, e)$$
$$= g_j(x, e) - \bar{g}_j(x), \qquad j = 1, \ldots, m, \quad (5.18)$$

and let

$$v(x, y, e) = U(x, y, e) - EU(x, y, e)$$
$$= U(x, y, e) - \overline{U}(x, y). \quad (5.19)$$

---

4. It is certainly a special way of defining "small uncertainty." However, it is more flexible than it may appear. If we want to deal with random variables for which different moments go to zero at different speeds, we can write $\epsilon e = \sum_{j=1}^{J} \epsilon^j v_j$, where the v_j, $j = 1, \ldots, J$, are appropriate zero-mean random variables.

When e has finite moments, as is implicitly assumed when we integrate utility functions over e, the random variables ϵe define a compact family of distributions in the sense of Samuelson (1970). A more general theory could be provided using compact families.

The certainty situation is defined by

$$\operatorname*{Max}_{x} \overline{U}[x, \bar{g}(x)]. \tag{5.20}$$

Let $\bar{x}$ be the solution of 5.20. To vary uncertainty we denote

$$g_j(x, e, \epsilon) = \bar{g}_j(x) + \epsilon\gamma_j(x, e), \qquad j = 1, \ldots, m, \tag{5.21}$$

$$U(x, y, e, \epsilon) = \overline{U}(x, y) + \epsilon v(x, y, e). \tag{5.22}$$

Let $x^*(\epsilon)$ be the solution of

$$\operatorname*{Max}_{x} U(x, g(x, e, \epsilon), e, \epsilon). \tag{5.23}$$

First-order certainty equivalence says that $x^*(\epsilon) - \bar{x}$ is of the order of ϵ^2. However, to define the certainty solution, we must now calculate $\bar{g}_j(x), j = 1, \ldots, m$, and $\overline{U}(x, y)$. If this is possible, intuitively it seems that this certainty equivalent will be a better approximation, since this problem is "closer" to the original problem. But beyond this intuitive insight not much can be said.

The choice of a particular certainty equivalent reflects a trade-off between the need for simplicity and the need for accuracy, but nothing very precise is given to guide us in this choice.

Using his concept of certainty equivalence, Malinvaud (1969a) obtains the following result.

Theorem 5.5. If the payoff function is twice differentiable and concave in the controlled and uncontrolled variables, increasing in the uncontrolled variables, if the functions defining the model are twice differentiable and strictly concave in the controlled variable, if the random variables are independent of instruments, if a solution exists in the certainty case, then first-order certainty equivalence holds in its neighborhood if the Hessian matrix of the payoff function is nonsingular in the certainty case.

The proof, which is a special case of the proof of theorem 6.1, is not given. The concavity assumptions of this theorem do not recognize the local character of the first-order certainty equivalence property. The main restrictions are differentiability conditions, as shown in theorem 5.5. However, they are not necessary, as Malinvaud (1969a) illustrates with examples.

To this theorem in a static world corresponds a theorem for the first period of an optimal strategy in a dynamic problem with increasing information. Consider the same dynamic setting as defined in the first section, where the model is now

$$y_1 = g_1(x_1, e_1),$$
$$y_2 = g_2(x_1, x_2, e_1, e_2),$$

$$.$$

$$.$$

$$.$$

$$y_T = g_T(x_1, \ldots, x_T, e_1, \ldots, e_T), \qquad (5.24)$$

with $y_t \epsilon R^m$, $x_t \epsilon R^n$, $t = 1, \ldots, T$, and where e_t is the p-vector $(e_t^1, \ldots, e_t^p)$ of real random variables $t = 1, \ldots, T$. Let $\Omega_t = R^p$ and $\Omega = \Pi_{t=1}^T \Omega_t$; the payoff function is

$$U(x, y, e) = U(x, y, e_1, \ldots, e_T). \qquad (5.25)$$

Let $f_t(e_t|e_{t-1}, \ldots, e_1)$ be the conditional probability density of e_t.

Theorem 5.6. Under the same assumptions as those in theorem 5.5, and if information increases with time, then in a stochastic dynamic programming problem first-order certainty equivalence holds for the first period of the sequential strategy.

Proof. We are looking for an optimal strategy,

$$\tilde{x}^* = [x_1^*, x_2^*(e_1), \ldots, x_T^*(e_1, \ldots, e_{T-1})],$$

which is the solution of the program

$$\text{Max}_x EU(x, g_1, \ldots, g_T, e_1, \ldots, e_T). \qquad (5.26)$$

For the general problem the first-order conditions, sufficient because of the concavity assumptions, are

$$\frac{\partial}{\partial x} \int_\Omega U[\tilde{x}^*, g(\tilde{x}^*, \epsilon e), \epsilon e_1, \ldots, \epsilon e_T]d\omega = 0, \quad (5.27)$$

with

$$d\omega = f_1(e_1)f_2(e_2|e_1) \ldots f_T(e_T|e_1, \ldots, e_{T-1})de_1 \ldots de_T$$

or

$$\frac{\partial}{\partial x_1} \int_\Omega U[\tilde{x}^*, g(\tilde{x}^*, \epsilon e), \epsilon e_1, \ldots, \epsilon e_T]d\omega = 0, \quad (5.28)$$

$$\frac{\partial}{\partial x_2(e_1)} \int_\Omega U[\tilde{x}^*, g(\tilde{x}^*, \epsilon e), \epsilon e][f_1(e_1)de_1]^{-1}d\omega = 0 \quad (5.29)$$

for each value of e_1, and so on until we have

$$\frac{\partial}{\partial x_T(e_1, \ldots, e_{T-1})} \int_\Omega U[\tilde{x}^*, g(\tilde{x}^*, \epsilon e), \epsilon e]$$
$$\times f_T(e_T|e_1, \ldots, e_{T-1})de_T = 0 \quad (5.30)$$

for each value of $e_1, \ldots, e_{T-1}$.

Differentiating[5] the first-order condition 5.28 at the certainty solution $\bar{x} = x^*$ ($\epsilon = 0$), we obtain

$$\sum_{h=1}^T \int_\Omega \frac{\partial^2 U}{\partial x_1 \partial x_h} (\bar{x}, g(\bar{x}, 0), 0)dx_h(e, 0)d\omega$$

$$+ \left(\sum_{i=1}^T \sum_{k=1}^p \int_\Omega \frac{\partial^2 U}{\partial x_1 \partial \epsilon^k} (\bar{x}, g(\bar{x}, 0), 0) e_i^k d\omega \right) d\epsilon = 0, \quad (5.31)$$

using the notation

$$\frac{\partial^2 U}{\partial x_1 \partial \epsilon^k} = \sum_{l=1}^T \frac{\partial^2 U}{\partial x_i \partial g_l} \frac{\partial g_l}{\partial \epsilon e_i^k} + \frac{\partial^2 U}{\partial x_i \partial \epsilon e_i^k}. \quad (5.32)$$

The second term of 5.31 is zero, as the following argument shows. Since

---

5. We assume when needed that we can differentiate under the integral operators.

$$\frac{\partial^2 U}{\partial x_1 \partial \epsilon^k} (\bar{x}, g(\bar{x}, 0), 0)$$

is not random, we can use the fact that

$$\int_{\Omega_1} e_i^k f_1(e_1) de_1 = 0, \quad \text{for } k = 1, \ldots, p. \tag{5.33}$$

Differentiation of 5.29 yields

$$\sum_{h=1}^{T} \int_{\Omega_2 \ldots \Omega_t} \frac{\partial^2 U}{\partial x_2 \partial x_h} (\bar{x}, g(\bar{x}, 0), 0) dx_h(e, 0)$$

$$\times f_2(e_2|e_1) \ldots f(e_T|e_1 \ldots e_{T-1}) de_2 \ldots de_T$$

$$+ \left[\sum_{i=1}^{T} \sum_{k=1}^{p} \int_{\Omega} \frac{\partial^2 U}{\partial x_2 \partial \epsilon^k} (\bar{x}, g(\bar{x}, 0), 0) e_i^k f_2(e_2|e_1) \cdot \right.$$

$$\left. f_T(e_T|e_1, \ldots, e_{T-1}) de_2 \ldots de_T \right] d\epsilon = 0 \tag{5.34}$$

for each value of e_1.

The second term of 5.34 can be rewritten as

$$\sum_{k=1}^{p} \frac{\partial^2 U^0}{\partial x_2 \partial \epsilon^k} \cdot e_1^k + \sum_{k=1}^{p} \sum_{i=2}^{T} \frac{\partial^2 U^0}{\partial x_2 \partial \epsilon^k} \int_{\Omega_2 \ldots \Omega_T} e_i^k f_2(e_2|e_1) \ldots$$

$$f(e_T|e_1, \ldots, e_{T-1}) de_2 \ldots de_T, \tag{5.35}$$

where the superscript zero means that the derivative is evaluated at the certainty point.

The second term of 5.35 is zero by the same argument used to show that the second term of 5.31 is zero.

Equation (5.34) is true for each value of e_1^k, $k = 1, \ldots, p$; taking the expected value with respect to e_1^k, we obtain

$$\sum_{h=1}^{T} \frac{\partial^2 U}{\partial x_2 \partial x_h} (\bar{x}, g(\bar{x}, 0), 0) \int_{\Omega} dx_h(e, 0) f(e) de = 0. \tag{5.36}$$

Similarly for $l = 2, \ldots, T$ we obtain

$$\sum_{h=1}^{T} \frac{\partial^2 U}{\partial x_l \partial x_h} (\bar{x}, g(\bar{x}, 0), 0) \int_{\Omega} dx_h(e, 0) f(e) de = 0. \quad (5.37)$$

Since the Hessian matrix of the payoff function is non-singular in the certainty case, we have from 5.31, 5.36, and 5.37 that

$$\int_{\Omega} dx_h(e, 0) f(e) de = 0 \quad \text{for each } h = 1, \ldots, T.$$

Hence $dx_1 = 0$. QED

6

Instrument-Dependent Randomness

First-Order Certainty Equivalence with Instrument-Dependent Randomness

In the literature on (first-order) certainty equivalence, the probability distributions of the random variables are assumed to be independent of the instruments. Under certain conditions this restriction is unnecessary, and we show the local character of the first-order certainty equivalence property. Then we proceed to a discussion of a different approach to the question of instrument-dependent randomness. We also give an intuitive explanation of the first-order certainty equivalence property and discuss the introduction of constraints on instruments.

We consider the static model of chapter 5 where the p-vector e of zero-mean random variables now has a probability density depending on instruments $f(e, x)$. Then the maximization problem is

$$\underset{x}{\text{Max}} \int_{\Omega} U[x, g(x, e), e]f(e, x)de \quad \text{with } \Omega = R^p. \quad (6.1)$$

The *certainty case* is defined by replacing the random variables e of problem 6.1 by their expected values. Since $Ee_k = 0$

for $k = 1, \ldots, p$, the certainty equivalent is obtained as the solution (assumed unique) of the problem:

$$\text{Max}_{x} \; U[x, g(x, 0), 0]. \tag{6.2}$$

As before, in order to vary the degree of uncertainty, we introduce a positive parameter ϵ and define the general problem

$$\text{Max}_{x} \int_{\Omega} U[x, g(x, \epsilon e), \epsilon e] f(e, x) de. \tag{6.3}$$

Theorem 6.1. If the payoff function $U(x, y, e)$ and the functions $g(x, e)$ defining the model are twice differentiable in all their variables, if the probability density of the random vector e is twice differentiable in the instruments, then when a unique optimal solution exists for the certainty case, first-order certainty equivalence holds if the Hessian matrix of the function $U[x, g(x, e), e]$ is nonsingular in the certainty case.[1]

1. Malinvaud (1969a) makes concavity assumptions to obtain a unique optimum continuous in ϵ. Since first-order certainty equivalence is a local property, we can say more generally that if a unique maximum exists for $\epsilon = 0$, then we satisfy the assumptions of the implicit function theorem (Dieudonné 1969, p. 277), which tells us that the optimal solution is continuous in ϵ in a neighborhood of $\epsilon = 0$. Second-order conditions are particularly difficult to obtain in our case. If x is a positive scalar, we can write them

$$\int_{\Omega} (U_{xx}f + 2U_x f_x + U f_{xx}) de < 0.$$

We can show that U is concave (and even strictly concave) under Malinvaud's assumption. Then $U_{xx} < 0$.

We can chose U to be positive and increasing in x, where $U > 0$, $U_x > 0$, U is increasing in e, and U_x is decreasing in e.

Let $\Omega = [0, +\infty)$. Sufficient conditions are that for some u and some v

$$f_x \leqq 0 \quad \text{for } e \leqq u, \qquad f_{xx} \geqq 0 \quad \text{for } e \leqq v,$$
$$f_x \geqq 0 \quad \text{for } e \geqq u, \qquad f_{xx} \leqq 0 \quad \text{for } e \geqq v,$$

$$\int_{\Omega} U_x f_x de = \int_{0}^{u} U_x f_x de + \int_{u}^{\infty} U_x f_x de \leqq U_x(x, u) \int_{0}^{\infty} f_x de = 0.$$

Similarly $\int_{\Omega} U f_{xx} de \leqq 0$.

Proof. The first-order conditions of the maximization problem defined in 6.3 are

$$\frac{\partial}{\partial x_i} \int_\Omega U[x, g(x, \epsilon e), \epsilon e] f(e, x) de = 0,$$

$$\text{for } i = 1, \ldots, n. \quad (6.4)$$

In a neighborhood of $\epsilon = 0$, the optimal solution x^* satisfies the first-order conditions because there is no constraint on x.

$$\int_\Omega \frac{\partial U}{\partial x_i} [x^*, g(x^*, \epsilon e)] f(e, x^*) de$$

$$+ \int_\Omega U[x^*, g(x^*, \epsilon e), \epsilon e] \frac{\partial f}{\partial x_i} (e, x^*) de = 0 \quad (6.5)$$

for $i = 1, \ldots, n$.

Differentiating we obtain, for $i = 1, \ldots, n$,

$$\sum_{h=1}^n \left[\int_\Omega \frac{\partial^2 U}{\partial x_i \partial x_h} [x^*, g(x^*, \epsilon e), \epsilon e] f(e, x^*) de \right.$$

$$+ \int_\Omega \frac{\partial U}{\partial x_i} [x^*, g(x^*, \epsilon e), \epsilon e] \frac{\partial f}{\partial x_h} (e, x^*) de$$

$$+ \int_\Omega \frac{\partial U}{\partial x_h} [x^*, g(x^*, \epsilon e), \epsilon e] \frac{\partial f}{\partial x_i} (e, x^*) de$$

$$\left. + \int_\Omega U[x^*, g(x^*, \epsilon e), \epsilon e] \frac{\partial^2 f}{\partial x_i \partial x_h} (e, x^*) de \right] dx_h^*$$

$$+ \left[\int_\Omega \frac{\partial^2 U}{\partial x_i \partial \epsilon} [x^*, g(x^*, \epsilon e), \epsilon e] f(e, x^*) de \right.$$

$$\left. + \int_\Omega \frac{\partial U}{\partial \epsilon} [x^*, g(x^*, \epsilon e), \epsilon e] \frac{\partial f}{\partial x_i} (e, x^*) de \right] d\epsilon = 0. \,(6.6)$$

If the differentiation is performed around the certainty point $\epsilon = 0$, $\bar{x} = x^*(0)$, and we have the following simplifications for each $i = 1, \ldots, n$. Since

$$\frac{\partial^2 U}{\partial x_i \partial x_h} [\bar{x}, g(\bar{x}, 0), 0]$$

is not random,

$$\int_\Omega \frac{\partial^2 U}{\partial x_i \partial x_h} [x^*, g(x^*, \epsilon e), \epsilon e] f(e, x^*) de$$

$$= \int_\Omega \frac{\partial^2 U}{\partial x_i \partial x_h} [\bar{x}, g(\bar{x}, 0), 0] f(e, \bar{x}) de$$

$$= \frac{\partial^2 U}{\partial x_i \partial x_h} [\bar{x}, g(\bar{x}, 0), 0] \int_\Omega f(e, \bar{x}) de. \quad (6.7)$$

Since $f(e, x)$ is a probability density on Ω, the right-hand side of equation 6.7 simplifies to

$$\frac{\partial^2 U}{\partial x_i \partial x_h} [\bar{x}, g(\bar{x}, 0), 0].$$

Similarly

$$\int_\Omega \frac{\partial U}{\partial x_i} [x^*, g(x^*, \epsilon e), \epsilon e] \frac{\partial f}{\partial x_h} (e, x^*) de$$

$$= \frac{\partial U}{\partial x_i} [\bar{x}, g(\bar{x}, 0), 0] \int_\Omega \frac{\partial f}{\partial x_h} (e, \bar{x}) de = 0, \quad (6.8)$$

because $\int_\Omega f(e, x) de = 1$ for each x implies

$$\int_\Omega \frac{\partial f}{\partial x_h} (e, \bar{x}) de = 0, \qquad \text{for } h = 1, \ldots, n.$$

Also we have

$$\int_\Omega U[x^*, g(x^*, \epsilon e), \epsilon e] \frac{\partial^2 f}{\partial x_i \partial x_h} (e, x^*) de$$

$$= U[\bar{x}, g(\bar{x}, 0), 0] \int_\Omega \frac{\partial^2 f}{\partial x_i \partial x_h} (e, \bar{x}) de = 0 \quad (6.9)$$

for $h = 1, \ldots, n$.

$$\int_\Omega \frac{\partial U}{\partial \epsilon} [x^*, g(x^*, \epsilon e), \epsilon e] \frac{\partial f}{\partial x_i} (e, x^*) de$$

$$= \sum_{k=1}^{p} \int_\Omega \left(\sum_{j=1}^{m} U_{2j} \frac{\partial g_j}{\partial \epsilon e_k} + U_{3k} \right) e_k \frac{\partial f}{\partial x_i} (e, x^*) de \quad (6.10)$$

where

$$U_{2j} = \frac{\partial U}{\partial y_j} [x^*, y^*, \epsilon e], \qquad j = 1, \ldots, m,$$

$$U_{3k} = \frac{\partial U}{\partial \epsilon e_k} [x^*, y^*, \epsilon e], \qquad k = 1, \ldots, p.$$

Evaluating the derivatives at the certainty point, we obtain

$$\sum_{k=1}^{p} \left(\sum_{j=1}^{m} U_{2j}^0 \frac{\partial g_j^0}{\partial \epsilon e_k} + U_{3k}^0 \right) \int_{\Omega} e_k \frac{\partial f}{\partial x_i} (e, \bar{x}) de. \qquad (6.11)$$

We know that for each x

$$\int_{\Omega} e_k \cdot f(e, x) de = 0, \qquad k = 1, \ldots, p.$$

Hence

$$\int_{\Omega} e_k \cdot \frac{\partial f}{\partial x_i} (e, x) de = 0, \qquad k = 1, \ldots, p.$$

In the same way

$$\int_{\Omega} \frac{\partial^2 U}{\partial x_i \partial \epsilon} [x^*, g(x^*, \epsilon e), \epsilon e] f(e, x^*) de = 0$$

then becomes

$$\sum_{h=1}^{n} \frac{\partial^2 U}{\partial x_i \partial x_h} [\bar{x}, g(\bar{x}, 0), 0] \cdot dx_h^* = 0, \qquad i = 1, \ldots, n. \quad (6.12)$$

Since by assumption the determinant of the matrix $((\partial^2 U / \partial x_i \partial x_h)[x, g(x, 0), 0])$ is nonzero, then $dx_h^* = 0$, $h = 1, \ldots, n$.   QED

Note that by redefining the random variables e it is always possible to formulate the problem with additive random disturbances in the model. Consider the following:

$$y = g(x, e).$$

Let $\bar{g}(x) = Eg(x, e)$ and $\bar{e} = g(x, e) - \bar{g}(x)$. Then

$$y = \bar{g}(x) + \bar{e} \quad \text{with } E\bar{e} = 0. \qquad (6.13)$$

Obviously no assumption of differentiability of g in e is then necessary. However, it should be clear that the certainty equivalent defined by 6.13 is now different from the certainty equivalent defined by 6.2. Note also that it will be more difficult to compute, since $g(x)$ must be evaluated.

In a special case, the generalized linear quadratic case, first-order certainty equivalence holds, and we give an explicit form for the second-order variation. The model is defined by

$$y = Rx + e$$

where $x \in R^n$ and e (and consequently y) are random variables with values in R^m and R is a fixed $m \times n$ matrix. Moreover $Ee = 0$ and

$$Eee' = \epsilon^2 \left[\sum_{i=1}^{m} \sum_{j=1}^{m} (x'V_{ij}x + w_{ij}'x + z_{ij})E_{ij} \right], \quad (6.14)$$

where E_{ij} is a $(m \times m)$ matrix of zeros with the (i, j) element equal to 1. For each $i = 1, \ldots, m, j = 1, \ldots, m$, V_{ij} is an $n \times n$ matrix, w_{ij} is an $n \times 1$ vector, z_{ij} is a scalar such that $V_{ij} = V_{ji}$, $w_{ij} = w_{ji}$, and $z_{ij} = z_{ji}$.

The payoff function is

$$U(x, y) = y'Ay + x'Bx + y'Cx + k'x + p'y,$$

where A, B, C, K, and p are constant matrices of conforming dimensions.

Let us first obtain the optimal solution.

$$U(x, Rx + e) = x'(R'AR + B + R'C)x + (k' + p'R)x$$
$$+ e'Cx + e'ARx + x'R'Ae + p'e + e'Ae,$$

$$EU(x, Rx + e) = x'(R'AR + B + R'C)x$$
$$+ (k' + p'R)x + E(e'Ae), \quad (6.15)$$

$$E(e'Ae) = E\mathrm{tr}e'Ae = E\mathrm{tr}ee'A = \mathrm{tr}(Eee')A$$
$$= \epsilon^2 \sum_{i=1}^{m} \sum_{j=1}^{m} (x'V_{ij}x + w_{ij}'x + z_{ij})\mathrm{tr}E_{ij}A.$$

But tr $E_{ij}A = a_{ij}$. So

$$E(e'Ae) = \epsilon^2 \sum_{j=1}^{m} \sum_{i=1}^{m} a_{ji}(x'V_{ij}x + w'_{ij}x + z_{ij})$$

$$= \epsilon^2 \left[x' \left(\sum_{i=1}^{m} \sum_{j=1}^{m} a_{ji}V_{ij} \right) x \right.$$

$$\left. + \left(\sum_{i=1}^{m} \sum_{j=1}^{m} a_{ji}w'_{ij} \right) x + \sum_{i=1}^{m} \sum_{j=1}^{m} a_{ji}z_{ij} \right].$$

If we let

$$\overline{V} = \sum_{i=1}^{m} \sum_{j=1}^{m} a_{ji}V_{ij},$$

$$\overline{w}' = \sum_{i=1}^{m} \sum_{j=1}^{m} a_{ji}w'_{ij},$$

$$\overline{z} = \sum_{i=1}^{m} \sum_{j=1}^{m} a_{ji}z_{ij},$$

then 6.15 becomes

$$EU(x, Rx + e) = x'(R'AR + B + R'C + \epsilon^2\overline{V})x$$
$$+ (k' + p'R + \epsilon^2\overline{w}')x + \epsilon^2\overline{z}. \quad (6.16)$$

The maximization of 6.16 with respect to x then gives

$$x^* = -\tfrac{1}{2}(R'AR + B + R'C + \epsilon^2\overline{V})^{-1}(k + R'p + \epsilon^2\overline{w}).$$

The assumption of the existence of a unique global optimum for $\epsilon = 0$ means here that $M = (R'AR + B + R'C)$ is negative definite,[2] so that $(R'AR + B + R'C + \epsilon^2\overline{V})$ is nega-

2. The literature lacks precision on this point. Consider the linear quadratic model without instrument dependence. When the quadratic term of the payoff function is said to be negative definite, it must be understood in the sense that $R'AR + B + R'C$, and not only A and B, must be negative definite. This assumption cannot be straightforwardly deduced from separate assumptions on the original payoff function and on the model. One simple case occurs when $C = 0$; then if A and B are negative definite, $R'AR + B$ is still negative definite. This weakness of second-order conditions appeared clearly in the formulation of the general model.

tive definite in a neighborhood of $\epsilon = 0$. The certainty equivalent obtained by setting $\epsilon = 0$ is then $x^0 = -\frac{1}{2}M^{-1}(k + R'p)$.

Observing that $(M + \epsilon^2\bar{V})^{-1} \approx M^{-1} - M^{-1}\epsilon^2\bar{V}M^{-1}$ for small ϵ, we have

$$x^* - x^0 \approx \frac{\epsilon^2}{2} M^{-1}[\bar{V}M^{-1}(k + R'p) - w]. \tag{6.17}$$

It has been argued that it is always possible to find a more fundamental random variable u independent of instruments and such that $e = h(x, u)$ with $Eu = 0$. Let $p(u)$ be the probability density of u. Then the maximization problem can be rewritten

$$\underset{x}{\text{Max}} \int U(x, g(x, h(x, u)), h(x, u))p(u)du. \tag{6.18}$$

Theorem 5.5 can be applied directly if $h(\cdot, u)$ is twice continuously differentiable. The certainty equivalent is then the solution of

$$\underset{x}{\text{Max}} \ U(x, g(x, h(x, 0)), h(x, 0)), \tag{6.19}$$

which is different from the certainty equivalent solution of

$$\underset{x}{\text{Max}} \ U(x, g(x, 0), 0), \tag{6.20}$$

since in general $Eh(x, u) \neq h(x, Eu)$.

Then why is there a need for theorem 6.1?

For the same intuitive reasons as those given in the second section of chapter 5, the certainty equivalent solution of 6.20 may be considered better than the one corresponding to 6.19, since 6.20 is "closer" to 6.1 than 6.19. In addition, and contrary to the previous situation, the model corresponding to 6.19 is in general much simpler that the one corresponding to 6.20, which in most cases is unknown even to the decision maker. These are the most fundamental reasons for proving the validity of the certainty equivalent corresponding to 6.19. More technically, the differentiability conditions may be satisfied for the model with instrument-dependent randomness and not for the more fundamental model, because the distribution of e is usually obtained as an integral from the distribution of u.

Before dealing with constraints on instruments in the first-order certainty equivalence framework, I shall give an intuitive explanation of the first-order certainty equivalence property in the simplest case.

The maximization problem can be reduced to

$$\text{Max}_{x \in R} \int_{\Omega} V(x, \, \epsilon e) f(e) de,$$

and the first-order condition is

$$\int_{\Omega} \frac{\partial V}{\partial x} (x, \, \epsilon e) f(e) de = 0.$$

Consider the optimal decision $\bar{x}$ in the certainty case and a small uncertainty represented by

$$\begin{aligned} e &= e_1 \quad \text{with probability } p(e_1), \\ &= e_2 \quad \text{with probability } p(e_2), \\ Ee &= 0. \end{aligned}$$

A variation dx of the optimal decision would be of no value, since to the first order

$$\begin{aligned} dU &= \frac{\partial V}{\partial x} (x, e_1) dx \quad \text{with probability } p(e_1), \\ &= \frac{\partial V}{\partial x} (x, e_2) dx \quad \text{with probability } p(e_2). \end{aligned}$$

Hence

$$EdU = \frac{\partial V}{\partial x} (x, e_1) dx p(e_1) + \frac{\partial V}{\partial x} (x, e_2) dx p(e_2).$$

Since e_1 and e_2 are small, we have

$$\begin{aligned} EdU &= \frac{\partial^2 V}{\partial x \partial e} (x, 0) e_1 dx p(e_1) + \frac{\partial^2 V}{\partial x \partial e} (x, 0) e_2 dx p(e_2) \\ &= \frac{\partial^2 V}{\partial x \partial e} (x, 0) dx [e_1 p(e_1) + e_2 p(e_2)] = 0. \end{aligned}$$

The effect of a change dx is, to the first order, as likely to have a positive effect as a negative effect.

The presence of instrument-dependent randomness does not change this conclusion. In such a case we have in EdU an additional term

$$V(x, 0) \frac{dp(e_1)}{dx} dx + V(x, 0) \frac{dp(e_2)}{dx} dx$$

$$= V(x, 0)dx \left[\frac{dp(e_1)}{dx} + \frac{dp(e_2)}{dx} \right] = 0,$$

since $p(e_1) + p(e_2) = 1$ for any x. Therefore no gain can be expected, to the first order, from a change dx of the optimal policy.

Finally we return to the question of constraints on instruments, first in the simplest static case.

$$\underset{x}{\text{Max}} \int_\Omega V(x, \epsilon e)f(e)de$$

subject to $h(x) \leq 0$ with h differentiable. The first-order condition is

$$\int_\Omega \frac{\partial V}{\partial x} (x, \epsilon e)f(e)de + \mu \frac{dh(x)}{dx} = 0.$$

Differentiating around the certainty case, we have

$$\left[\frac{\partial^2 V}{\partial x^2} (\bar{x}, 0) + \mu \frac{d^2 h(\bar{x})}{dx^2} \right] dx + \frac{dh(\bar{x})}{dx} \cdot d\mu = 0.$$

Now suppose that $dx \neq 0$; then we have

$$\left[\frac{\partial^2 V}{\partial x^2} (\bar{x}, 0) + \mu \frac{d^2 h(\bar{x})}{dx^2} \right] (dx)^2 + \frac{dh(\bar{x})}{dx} d\mu dx = 0.$$

But $(dh(\bar{x})/dx)dxd\mu = 0$ in all cases.

If $h(\bar{x}) < 0$, then $h(\bar{x} + d\bar{x}) < 0$ by continuity, so $\mu = 0$ and $\mu + d\mu = 0$, implying $d\mu = 0$. If $h(\bar{x}) = 0$ and $h(\bar{x} + dx) = 0$, then $(dh(\bar{x})/dx)dx = 0$. Finally, if $h(\bar{x}) = 0$ and $h(\bar{x} + dx) < 0$ for any dx, then $\mu = 0$. Therefore binding constraints on instruments of the first period of a dynamic maximization problem are admissible. See Malinvaud (1969b) for this argument in a more general framework.

However, constraints on future values of instruments may lead to the breakdown of the first-order certainty equivalence property for the first period. Indeed, it is sufficient to reinterpret Sandee's example with ϵ small to see that the variation in the optimal policy is of the order of ϵ and not ϵ^2.

Irreversibility can be viewed as a special case of a constraint on instruments in future periods. The quantity of forests at date $t + 1$ is bounded above by the quantity of forests we keep at date t; that is, $x_{t+1} \leq x_t$. For this reason certainty equivalents or first-order certainty equivalents cannot in general be used in these situations. Further work has been devoted to the study of cases in which the use of certainty equivalents induces a bias in favor of irreversible investment (Arrow and Fisher 1974, Henry 1974).

Some Economic Applications

The result on first-order certainty equivalence with instrument-dependent randomness can be applied to a number of interesting questions in many fields of economic theory. It is relevant in the numerous cases in which economic agents, by their behavior, modify subjective or objective probabilities involved in their maximization problems. In each of the following examples we show how certainty equivalence holds, and we discuss the difficult question of the sign and structure of second-order variation.

FULL EMPLOYMENT FISCAL POLICY IN THE LONG RUN

The problem in straightforward notation is formalized as

$$\text{Max} - (Y - Y_0)^2,$$

subject to

$$Y = aG + e, \qquad a > 0$$
$$Ee = 0, \qquad \text{var } e = \epsilon^2 G^2,$$

where Y is gross national product and G is government spending. The problem arises from the countervailing effects of government spending: an increase in production on the one hand, an increase in instability of outcomes on the other.

The certainty equivalent government spending is $\overline{G} = Y_0/a$. The optimal government spending is obtained from

$$\frac{dE}{dG}[a^2G^2 + Y_0^2 + e^2 + 2aGe - 2aGY_0 - 2eY_0] = 0,$$

$$G^* = \frac{aY_0}{a^2 + \epsilon^2} \approx \overline{G} - \frac{\epsilon^2 Y_0}{a^3}, \text{ if } \epsilon \text{ is small.}$$

Increased uncertainty in the neighborhood of the certainty case will induce a more conservative policy, which in some sense justifies the rule of thumb that the more the action can destabilize the system, the more conservative one should be. If, on the contrary, the action is thought to increase stability (by an increase of government action instead of decentralized actions), the opposite result is obtained; for example, if

$$\text{var } e = \epsilon^2(G_{\max}^2 - G^2) \quad \text{with } G_{\max} \gg Y_0/a,$$

then

$$G^* \approx \overline{G} + \epsilon^2 Y_0/a^3.$$

Optimal spending is enlarged by its effect on uncertainty reduction.

FISCAL OR MONETARY POLICY

Let M be money in circulation and Y be GNP. Then M_0 and Y_0 are the targets for money and GNP. Moreover, M and Y are linearly related to the government spending and the interest rate, which are the instruments. The optimal policy is obtained by solving the following problem:

$$\text{Max} - (Y - Y_0)^2 - (M - M_0)^2, \quad Eu = 0, \text{ var } u = \epsilon^2 \cdot \alpha^2 G^2,$$

subject to

$$Y = aG + br + u, \qquad\qquad Ev = 0, \text{ var } v = \epsilon^2 \cdot \beta^2 r^2,$$
$$M = cG + dr + v, \qquad\qquad\qquad \text{cov } (u, v) = 0.$$

The certainty equivalent policy is

$$\overline{G} = \frac{(aY_0 + cM_0)(b^2 + d^2) - (bY_0 + dM_0)(ab + cd)}{\Delta},$$

$$\overline{r} = \frac{(bY_0 + dM_0)(a^2 + c^2) - (aY_0 + cM_0)(ab + cd)}{\Delta},$$

under the assumption that $\Delta = (a^2 + c^2)(b^2 + d^2) - (ab + cd)^2 = (ad - cb)^2 \neq 0$.

Using the result of the quadratic case, we have

$$G^* = \overline{G} - \frac{\epsilon^2}{\Delta}[\alpha^2 G^0(b^2 + d^2) - \beta^2 r^0(ab + cd)],$$

$$r^* = \overline{r} - \frac{\epsilon^2}{\Delta}[\beta^2 r^0(a^2 + c^2) - \alpha^2 G^0(ab + cd)].$$

The term $(ab + cd)$ can be expected to be negative, so that uncertainty leads to conservative policy in the same way as before. The greater the destabilization effects (the greater α^2 and β^2), the more conservative one should be.

If, on the contrary, var $u = \epsilon^2\alpha^2 (G - G_{min})^2$ with G^0 (and r^0) much smaller than G_{min}, and if we note $\beta^2 = k\alpha^2$, then we obtain

$$G^* \approx \overline{G} - \frac{\epsilon^2\alpha^2}{\Delta}[(\overline{G} - G_{min})(b^2 + d^2) - k(ab + cd)\overline{r}],$$

$$r^* \approx \overline{r} - \frac{\epsilon^2\alpha^2}{\Delta}[\overline{G}(b^2 + d^2) - k(ab + cd)(\overline{r} - G_{min})].$$

Now the instrument G is stabilizing, and the instrument r remains destabilizing. If k is small, an increase of uncertainty leads to an increase of G and to a decrease of r. The stabilizing role of G is overwhelming. If k becomes larger, we reach a point at which G^* and r^* are both larger than their certainty equivalents. When k becomes large with respect to $G_{min} - G^0$, that is, the instability in the income equation is smaller than in the money equation, then r^* becomes larger than r^0 and G less than G^0. This is due to the interactions of the model. (If $b = c = 0$, this phenomenon does not occur.)

It then appears that the signs of second-order variations

are difficult to predict, and that the trade-off between risk aversion and the instrument effect may be quite complex.

EXAMPLES IN MICROECONOMICS

Individual behavior of economic agents under uncertainty offers a large variety of cases in which objective or subjective probability densities depend on control variables. For example, the monopolist attempts to influence the probability distribution of his sales, and the insured person by preventive care modifies his probability of becoming sick, inducing a moral hazard problem.

We shall discuss the example of a consumer who can influence the probability of his future random income. We use a two-period model. The consumer has a utility function chosen to be quadratic for simplicity in spite of its well-known undesirable characteristic of increasing aversion for risk.

$$U(c_1, c_2) = -(c_1 - a)^2 - (c_2 - b)^2,$$
$$c_1 = Y_1 - s_1,$$
$$c_2 = Y_2 + s_1(1 + r),$$

where Y_1 and Y_2 are the sure incomes of periods 1 and 2, s_1 is the saving of period 1, and r the interest rate.

If $r = r_0$ is not random, the maximization of U gives

$$\bar{s}_1 = \frac{Y_1 - a - (Y_2 - b)(1 + r_0)}{1 + (1 + r_0)^2}.$$

If r is now a random variable with mean r_0 and standard error $\epsilon\sigma$, then when ϵ is small the maximization of $EU(c_1, c_2)$ gives

$$s_1^* \approx \bar{s}_1 \left(1 - \frac{\epsilon^2\sigma^2}{1 + (1 + r_0)^2}\right).$$

Risk aversion leads to a decrease of savings, as expected from Sandmo (1970). Now assume that the variance of the return is a decreasing function of the amount saved, $\text{var } r = \epsilon^2\sigma^2(\bar{s} + (\lambda^2/s_1))$. This special form is, again for simplicity,

$$s_1^* \approx \bar{s}_1 \left(1 - \frac{\epsilon^2 \sigma^2 \bar{s}}{1 + (1 + r_0)^2} \right) + \frac{\lambda^2}{2} \cdot \frac{\epsilon^2 \sigma^2}{1 + (1 + r_0)^2}.$$

Here we have two effects, the negative effect due to risk aversion and the positive one due to the instrument effect. If we had a utility function with risk preference, and the variance of the interest rate was an increasing function of the amount saved (var $r = \epsilon^2 \sigma^2 (\bar{s} - \lambda^2/s_1)$), then the uncertainty effect would increase saving, but the instrument effect would decrease this supplementary saving. In these cases the certainty equivalent is a still better approximation to the optimal solution.

Toward a More General First-Order Equivalence

Consider the following maximization problem:

$$\underset{x}{\text{Max }} EU(x, y, e)$$

subject to

$$y = g(x, e), \tag{6.21}$$

where the random variables e can be decomposed as $e = h(v, w)$ and v, w are two independent[3] zero-mean random vectors with probability densities $f_1(v, x)$, $f_2(w, x)$ which can depend on the instruments x. Assume h to be differentiable.

We introduce the positive parameter ϵ to vary uncertainty in the following way: $e = h(v, \epsilon w)$. The reference problem is now defined with $\epsilon = 0$ or $e = h(v, 0)$ instead of the certainty problem employed in the previous approach. We assume that a unique solution exists for problem 6.21 when $\epsilon = 0$. Moreover we know how to compute the solution for $\epsilon = 0$. Let $x^0 = x^*(0)$ denote this solution.

The generalization of this section says that under the assumptions of our theorem, the differentiability of h, and the twice differentiability of the probability densities f_1 and f_2 in

---

3. Independence is not really necessary. It is sufficient to have $\int_\Omega w f(w|v) dw = 0$ for all v, where $f(w|v)$ is the conditional probability of w given v.

the instruments, the solution of problem 6.21 is the same to the first order as the solution x^0 of the reference problem, in the neighborhood of $\epsilon = 0$.

We sketch the proof, which is similar to the proof in the first section.

$$\underset{x}{\text{Max}} \int_{\Omega_v} \int_{\Omega_w} U[x, g(x, h(v, \epsilon w)), h(v, \epsilon w)]$$

$$\cdot f_1(v, x) \cdot f_2(w, x) dv dw,$$

where

$\Omega_v = R^l$ if v is a random vector with values in R^l,

$\Omega_w = R^p$ if w is a random vector with values in R^p.

The first-order conditions are

$$\frac{\partial}{\partial x_i} \int_{\Omega_v} \int_{\Omega_w} U[x, g(x, h(v, \epsilon w)), h(v, \epsilon w)]$$

$$\cdot f_1(v, x) \cdot f_2(w, x) dv dw = 0, \qquad i = 1, \ldots, n.$$

We differentiate these equations at $\epsilon = 0$, $x = x^0$, and by arguments similar to those in the first section we obtain

$$\sum_{h=1}^{n} \int_{\Omega_v} \left[\frac{\partial^2 U}{\partial x_i \partial x_h} [x^0, g(x^0, h(v, 0)), h(v, 0)] f_1(v, x^0) \right.$$

$$+ \frac{\partial U}{\partial x_i} [x^0, g(x^0, h(v, 0)), h(v, 0)] \cdot \frac{\partial f_1}{\partial x_h} (v, x^0)$$

$$+ \frac{\partial U}{\partial x_h} [x^0, g(x^0, h(v, 0)), h(v, 0)] \cdot \frac{\partial f_1}{\partial x_i} (v, x^0)$$

$$+ U[x^0, g(x^0, h(v, 0)), h(v, 0)]$$

$$\left. \cdot \frac{\partial^2 f_1}{\partial x_i \partial x_h} (v, x^0) dv \right] \cdot dx_h^* = 0, \qquad i = 1, \ldots, n.$$

If the determinant of the matrix

$$\int_{\Omega_v} \left(\frac{\partial^2 U^0}{\partial x_i \partial x_h} \cdot f_1^0 + \frac{\partial U^0}{\partial x_i} \cdot \frac{\partial f_1^0}{\partial x_h} + \frac{\partial U^0}{\partial x_h} \cdot \frac{\partial f_1^0}{\partial x_i} + U^0 \frac{\partial^2 f_1^0}{\partial x_i \partial x_h} \right) dv$$

is nonzero, then $dx_h^* = 0$ $(h = 1, \ldots, n)$ and first-order equivalence holds.

This result may be important in the following sense. If we know how to solve a stochastic maximization problem with given probability distributions, we have to a first-order approximation the solution of problems in which these probability distributions are perturbed by small random variables (consider, for example, $e = v + \epsilon w$).

An alternative formulation of first-order certainty equivalence is to say that the derivative of the objective function with respect to ϵ, evaluated at the certainty situation, is zero. This point is obvious since the derivative of the optimal action with respect to ϵ is then zero. An immediate application of this observation in the dynamic setting yields a result derived by Radner and Stiglitz (1976) concerning the value of information.

In the following, differentiability is assumed whenever necessary.

Consider the simple maximization problem

$$\underset{x \in R}{\text{Max}} \int_R U(x, e) f(e) de, \tag{6.22}$$

where $f(e)$ is to be interpreted as the prior distribution of the agent about the random variable e. The agent can also buy information—the right to observe a signal $s \in S$—whose probability distribution depends on the value of e. In addition these distributions $p(s|e, \epsilon)$ are indexed by a parameter ϵ such that $\epsilon = 0$ corresponds to a noninformative signal; that is, for any $s_1 \in S$, $p(s = s_1|e, 0)$ is independent of e.

After observing s, the agent maximizes his expected utility, using his posterior distribution over e:

$$f(e|s, \epsilon) = \frac{p(s|e, \epsilon) f(e)}{p(s, \epsilon)};$$

that is,

$$\underset{x \in R}{\text{Max}} \int_R U(x, e) f(e|s, \epsilon) de,$$

giving the optimal response function $x(s, \epsilon)$. The expected utility of this course of action is

$$V(\epsilon) = \int_S \int_R U(x(s, \epsilon))f(e|s, \epsilon)dep(s)ds. \qquad (6.23)$$

The random variable s can be written $s = s_0 + \epsilon\varphi$, where s_0 is a random variable independent of e and φ is a random variable correlated with e. The case $\epsilon = 0$ is clearly the case without information.

We know that generalized first-order certainty equivalence holds at $\epsilon = 0$. Hence

$$\frac{dV}{d\epsilon}(\epsilon = 0) = 0.$$

Therefore the derivative of the value of information $(6.23 - 6.22)$ at no information $\epsilon = 0$ is zero.

As observed by Radner and Stiglitz (1976), this implies (when the marginal cost of information is strictly positive at $\epsilon = 0$) a nonconcavity in the value of information when information eventually becomes valuable.

References

AKERLOF, G. A. 1970. The market for "lemons": Quality uncertainty and the market mechanism. *Quarterly Journal of Economics* 84: 488–500.

ARROW, K. J. 1963–1964. The role of securities in the optimal allocation of risk-bearing. *Review of Economic Studies* 41: 91–96.

—— 1963. Uncertainty and the welfare economics of medical care. *American Economic Review* 53: 941–973.

—— 1968. The economics of moral hazard: Further comment. *American Economic Review* 58: 537–539.

—— 1973. Social responsibility and economic efficiency. *Public Policy* 21: 1–18.

—— 1974. Optimal insurance and generalized deductibles. *Scandinavian Actuarial Journal* 10: 1–42.

ARROW, K. J., and DEBREU, G. 1954. Existence of equilibrium for a competitive economy. *Econometrica* 22: 265–290.

ARROW, K. J., and FISHER, A. C. 1974. Environmental preservation, uncertainty and irreversibility. *Quarterly Journal of Economics* 88: 312–319.

ARROW, K. J., and GREEN, J. R. 1973. Notes on expectations equilibria in bayesian settings. Working paper no. 33, Stanford University.

ARROW, K. J., and HAHN, F. H. 1971. *General competitive analysis.* San Francisco: Holden-Day.

AUMANN, R. J. 1964. Markets with a continuum of traders. *Econometrica* 32: 39–50.

BEWLEY, T. F. 1973. Edgeworth's conjecture. *Econometrica* 41: 425–454.

BROWN, D. G., and ROBINSON, A. 1972. A limit theorem on the cores of large standard exchange economies. *Proceedings of the National Academy of Sciences* 69: 1258–60.

CELLINA, A. 1969. A theorem on the approximation of compact multivalued mappings. *Rendiconte della Academia Nazionale dei Liniei* 429–433.

DEBREU, G. 1959. *Theory of value.* New York: J. Wiley and Sons.

DEBREU, G., and SCARF, H. 1963. A limit theorem on the core of an economy. *International Economic Review* 4: 235–246.

DIAMOND, P. A. 1967. The role of the stock market in a general equilibrium model with technological uncertainty. *American Economic Review* 57: 759–776.

DIEUDONNÉ, J. 1969. *Elements d'analyse,* vol. 1. Paris: Gauthier-Villars.

DUNFORD, N., and SCHWARTZ, J. 1963. *Linear operators.* New York: Interscience.

EDGEWORTH, F. Y. 1881. *Mathematical psychics.* London: Kegan Paul.

EHRLICH, I., and BECKER, G. S. 1972. Market insurance, self-insurance and self protection. *Journal of Political Economy* 80: 623–648.

GILLIES, D. B. 1959. *Solutions to general non-zero-sum games.* Contributions to the Theory of Games, vol. 4. ed. R. D. Luce and A. W. Tucker. Princeton, N.J.: Princeton University Press.

GOULD, J. P. 1969. The expected utility hypothesis and the selection of optimal deductibles for a given insurance policy. *Journal of Business* 42: 143–151.

GRANDMONT, J. M. 1972. Continuity properties of a Von Neumann–Morgenstern utility. *Journal of Economic Theory* 4: 45–57.

———— 1973. On the short-run equilibrium in a monetary economy. In *Allocation under uncertainty, equilibrium and optimality,* ed. J. Drèze. London: MacMillan.

GRANDMONT, J. M., and YOUNÈS, Y. 1972. On the efficiency of a monetary equilibrium. *Cepremap discussion paper.* Paris.

GREEN, J. R. 1971. Temporary general equilibrium in a sequential trading model with spot and future transactions. Core discussion paper no. 7127. Université de Louvain, Belgium.

———— 1972. On the inequitable nature of core allocations. *Journal of Economic Theory* 4: 132–143.

GREEN, J. R., and SHESHINSKI, E. 1973. Competitive inefficiencies in the presence of constrained transactions. Technical report no. 105, Stanford University.

HENRY, C. 1974. Option values in the economics of irreplaceable assets. *The Review of Economic Studies Symposium,* 89–104.

HILDENBRAND, W. 1974. *Core and equilibria in a large economy.* Princeton, N.J.: Princeton University Press.

HILDENBRAND, W., and KIRMAN, A. P. 1973. Size removes inequity. *Review of Economic Studies* 40: 305–320.

HILDENBRAND, W., SCHMEIDLER, D., and ZAMIR, S. 1971. Existence of approximate equilibria and cores. Core discussion paper no. 7119. Université de Louvain, Belgium.

HIRSCHLEIFER, J. 1970. *Investment, interest and capital.* Englewood Cliffs, N.J.: Prentice-Hall.

———— 1971. The private and social value of information and the reward to inventive activity. *American Economic Review* 61: 561–574.

KELLEY, J. L. 1970. *General topology.* New York: Van Nostrand.

KUHN, THOMAS S. 1962. *The Structure of Scientific Revolutions.* Chicago: University of Chicago Press.

LUCE, R. D., and RAIFFA, M. 1957. *Games and decisions.* New York: J. Wiley and Sons.

MALINVAUD, E. 1969a. Décisions en face de l'aléatoire et situation certaine approximativement équivalente. *Cahiers du Séminaire d'Econométrie* 11: 37–50.

———— 1969b. First-order certainty equivalence. *Econometrica* 37: 706–718.

———— 1972. The allocation of individual risks in large markets. *Journal of Economic Theory* 5: 312–328.

———— 1973. Markets of an exchange economy with individual risks. *Econometrica* 41: 383–410.

MOSSIN, J. 1968. Aspects of rational insurance purchasing. *Journal of Political Economy* 76: 553–568.

PARTHASARATHY, K. R. 1967. *Probability measures in metric spaces.* New York: Academic Press.

PASHIGIAN, B. P., SCHKADE, L. L., and MENEFEE, G. H. 1966. The selection of an optimal deductible for a given insurance policy. *Journal of Business* 39: 35–44.

PAULY, M. V. 1968. The economics of moral hazard. *American Economic Review* 58: 31–58.

———— 1974. Overinsurance and public provision of insurance: The roles of moral hazard and adverse selection. *Quarterly Journal of Economics* 88: 44–62.

POSNER, R. A. 1972. *Economic analysis of law.* Boston: Little, Brown and Co.

RADNER, R. 1968. Competitive equilibrium under uncertainty. *Econometrica* 36: 31–58.

RADNER, R., and STIGLITZ, J. E. 1976. A nonconcavity in the value of information. Mimeographed.

ROTHSCHILD, M., and STIGLITZ, J. E. 1973. Equilibrium in competitive insurance markets: The economics of imperfect information. Mimeographed.

SAMUELSON, P. A. 1970. The fundamental approximation theorem of portfolio analysis in terms of means, variances and higher moments. *Review of Economic Studies* 37: 537–542.

SANDMO, H. 1970. The effect of uncertainty on saving decision. *Review of Economic Studies* 37: 353–360.

SAVAGE, L. J. 1954. *The foundations of statistics.* New York: J. Wiley and Sons.

SCARF, H. 1967. The core of an *N*-person game. *Econometrica* 35: 50–69.

SHAPLEY, L. S., and SHUBIK, M. 1966. Quasi-cores in a monetary economy with nonconvex preferences. *Econometrica* 34: 805–827.

——— 1969. On the core of an economic system with externalities. *American Economic Review* 59: 678–684.

SIMON, H. 1956. Dynamic programming under uncertainty with a quadratic criterion function. *Econometrica* 24: 74–81.

SMITH, V. L. 1968. Optimal insurance coverage. *Journal of Political Economy* 75: 68–77.

STARR, R. M. 1969. Quasi-equilibrium in markets with non-convex preferences. *Econometrica* 37: 25–38.

——— 1973. Optimal production and allocation under uncertainty. *Quarterly Journal of Economics* 87: 81–95.

STARRETT, D. 1973a. Neutrality of money and the long-run Phillips curve. Harvard Institute of Economic Research, discussion paper no. 268.

——— 1973b. A note on externalities and the core. *Econometrica* 41: 179–183.

THEIL, H. 1954. Econometric models and welfare maximization. *Weltwirtschafthches Archiv* 72: 60–83.

——— 1957. A note on certainty equivalence in dynamic planning. *Econometrica* 25: 346–349.

——— 1958. *Economic forecasts and policy.* Amsterdam: North-Holland Publishing Co.

——— 1964. *Optimal decision rules for government and industry.* Amsterdam: North-Holland Publishing Co.

TINBERGEN, J. 1952. *On the theory of economic policy.* Amsterdam: North-Holland Publishing Co.

Index